Programming with MFC
& Visual C++ 6.0

Electrical and Electronic Engineering Design Series
Electric Circuits Analysis and Design

Electronic Circuit Design   with Bipolar and MOS Transistors

CMOS Circuit Design Analog, Digital, IC Layout

Digital Design Logic, Memory, Computers

Analog Filter Design

Error Correction Code Design

Computer Science Design Series
Programming with MFC & Visual C++ 6.0

Mathematics
Arithmetic – Integers, Fractions, Decimals

Algebra – A Clear Presentation

Programming with MFC & Visual C++ 6.0

Nicholas L. Pappas, Ph.D.

A Message about this Text: The subject is essentially endless. The purpose here is to say enough about the subject so that you, the reader, have a running start when you apply this knowledge to your work.

Knowing how to program in C, C++, C# expedites programming with MFC. However, knowing very little about programming in C, C++, & C# we show how, *with significant effort,* one can get a good head start programming with MFC.

The required accessory to the text is Visual C++ 6.0 (or later version). And, Jeff Prosise's text "Programming Windows with MFC" is, as a practical matter, a required yet optional accessory.

These efforts provide *startup* work experience. Once you have some work experience we are confident that you will be able to expand your know how with reasonable effort.

A Message from the Author: I have worked continuously in the electronics industry since 1950 except for 11 semesters teaching at San Jose State University (Professor and Chair Computer Engineering 1988-1993). There I discovered my talent for teaching such as it may be. After War2 I attended Lehigh University, and then transferred to Stanford where I earned the MS degree and, while working at HP in the early 1950's, the Ph.D. EE degree. (Somehow I did not get the word and formally apply for the BS degree.) Hardware design has been my principal activity. I learned enough about assembly language, Forth, C and C++ to design the software I needed for my projects. My current activity is designing integrated circuits.

Preface

This is about how to use Windows MFC[1] and Visual C++ 6.0[2] to write programs using windows without knowing how to write the complex code that produces the windows. The MFC/6.0 combination immensely simplifies the writing of any program that uses one or more windows.

Second, this is about learning how program with MFC from the bottom up so that you can produce the projects presented here. Many MFC classes and functions replace/obsolete many C, C++, and C# classes and functions. Consequently you can go directly to MFC, and save a lot of time and energy. Programming with MFC allows you to work at the top of the C hierarchy, while avoiding the limitations of C, C++, and C#.

> MFC statistics: The Microsoft Visual C++ MFC Library Reference Parts 1 and 2, The Class Library Reference, has 2968 pages of text and a 100 page index. The Table of Contents shows 217 Classes. There are many hundreds of functions. We do not know anything about the Parts 3, 4, 5 of this 5 volume set.

This text *begins* to show you how to program with MFC by using Visual C++ 6.0 to produce skeleton programs on the Visual C++ screen. Skeletons that include code producing the windows in which your programs will be presented. For example, skeletons that require adding only one code line to produce the "Hello World" program in a window.

We say *begin*, because learning how to program in any language is an endless task.

There is an unavoidable "cook book" element to using Visual C++ 6.0 that dictates how to create the skeletons, and where to enter your code in the skeletons.

This text is different. Instead of referring you to code on a disk (with few if any comments), and instead of offering partial explanations in the text, requiring you have to go back and forth from book to disk, and wondering what to do next, we show you how code is written that

---

[1] Microsoft Foundation Classes
[2] A Microsoft software program

actually creates programs that run on any computer using the windows operating system. That is why only the Visual C++ 6.0 disk is required.

We *briefly* explain most of the code lines used to produce the functions required by the projects. We expect you to have a basic programming capability.

This text uses the Jeff Prosise text[3] as a very useful reference.

Most of the time, JP's text tells us what functions to use. The MFC library, included with Visual C++, tells us how to use them (sometimes).

Once a skeleton program is created [JP213] [4], the next problem surfaced. We knew we wanted functions to do such and such, but do they exist in MFC or do we have to create them? As will become clear later some do exist, and some we had to write in order to implement *message handlers*.

With Jeff Prosise's text supporting us we were able to write programs using windows, while knowing nothing about windows programming and very little about MFC and the various C languages. JP's text gave us a great start with the design process producing programs presented in one or more windows.

That experience brings us to this point. We wrote this text, because even with the JP reference we learned that we had to answer many "How-do-we-do-that?" questions. Answers we needed in order to produce programs that run. Answers we share with you by presenting selected topics in the form of working projects.

Many types of programs can be implemented with MFC. We focus on dot exe (name.exe) executing programs.

> JP's text makes very clear the fact that there is much, much more to MFC then what we present here.

---

[3] Jeff Prosise, "Programming Windows with MFC", Second Edition,. ISBN 1572 316 950

[4] [JP213] means go to page 213 of JP's text.

As you read this text it is necessary that the Microsoft Visual C++ 6.0 program, or a later version, is up and running. We strongly recommend that JP's text is right there next to you.

Emphasis: The Visual C++ program, supported by the MFC, immensely facilitates (windows) program design.

A Note about Compilation errors When errors occur while building (compiling) a program in Visual C++ 6.0 the reasons why appear in the output pane of the Visual C++ 6.0 screen display. The reasons why may be numerous and many appear to be weird. This can happen when a merely a semicolon is omitted at the end of a statement.

Therefore, always build a program to check for errors EVERY TIME YOU ADD A CODE LINE so that you know where to look.

We have never had to use the debug facility by building every time we added one or more lines simply because the error(s) had to be in the line(s) we just added.

Our blog *npappasee.blogspot.com* may offer you additional information. Take a look.

We would appreciate receiving your comments and views on this text at *npappasz@yahoo.com*.

All of the code in this book is protected by copyright. You will create programs using the code as part of the process learning how to use Visual C++ 6.0. Using the programs for commercial gain is a no-no.

Contents

1 How Visual C++ Works

Visual C++ creates a workspace (a folder) that contains the set of code files that define the *code skeleton* of a project. The set of files is a working skeleton to which you will add code to create a functioning project.

Two wizards, AppWizard and ClassWizard, are the Visual C++ code generators. AppWizard creates the working skeleton code of a Windows application with features you specify via dialog boxes produced by AppWizard. When creating workspaces we make choices of the available options. Your choices may be different given the needs of your project.

ClassWizard facilitates adding new classes, new variables, as well as assist you in other code writing procedures. ClassWizard is used and explained in later chapters where projects are implemented.

The focus here is on creating executable files with the dot exe extension. There are three types of dot exe projects to choose from. We will Create one of each.

First create a folder in your directory in which your project files will be stored. We named the folder *Project X*.

Second open Visual C++ to get a Window containing three empty panes, tool bars and a status bar. The third pane, the output pane, may not present. To see the output pane click on *View*, click on *Output*.

1.1 Single document/view

1 Click *File*. Click *New* to get the *New* dialog box [JP213], which has 4 tabs. Select the *Projects* page tab. The page contains a list of project types you can create. Highlight *MfcAppWizard(exe)*. (Executing files, dot exe files, are produced by *MfcAppWizard(exe)*.)

2 In the *Projects* page (of the *New* dialog box) click on the small "box" to the right of the *Location* edit box.

This opens the *Choose Directory* dialog box. In the *Drives* box select the drive that stores *Project X*. In the *Directory name* box select the folder *Project X* that you want to store your project folders in. Click on *OK* to exit the *Choose Directory* dialog box, and return to *New*.

In the *Project name* edit box (of the *New* dialog box) type the project name *OneDoc*. (Note the addition of *OneDoc* to the path in the *Location* edit box.)

Observe that *Create new workspace* has been selected, and that the *Platform* is Win32.

Click OK. This opens the AppWizard by opening the *MFC AppWizard - Step 1* screen. The *OneDoc* folder has been created. Take a look in folder *Project X*.

From here on you are using AppWizard

01) In the *MFC AppWizard - Step 1* screen - select Single document., accept *Document/View architecture support*, and select your language. Click Next.

02) In the *MFC AppWizard - Step 2 of 6* screen change nothing. Database support not required. Click Next.

03) In the *MFC AppWizard - Step 3 of 6* screen uncheck *ActiveX Controls*. Click Next.

04) In the *MFC AppWizard - Step 4 of 6* screen uncheck 4 boxes. Increase number of files to 10. Click Next.

05) In the *MFC AppWizard - Step 5 of 6* screen click Next.

06) In the *MFC AppWizard - Step 6 of 6* screen click Finish.

07) In the *New Project Information* dialog box click *OK* to enter the *OneDoc* workspace.

You are done - the *OneDoc* workspace has been created on screen. In the left pane you can examine the project classes, resources, and files. Go to Section 1.4. When you are done *Click File*, click *Close Workspace*.

1.2 Multiple document/view

Do Single document/view steps 1 and 2 to create project *ManyDoc*.

11) In the *MFC AppWizard - Step 1* screen - select *Multiple documents*, accept *Document/View architecture support*, and select your language. Click Next.

12) In the *MFC AppWizard - Step 2 of 6* screen change nothing. Database support not required. Click Next.

13) In the *MFC AppWizard - Step 3 of 6* screen uncheck *ActiveX Controls*. Click Next.

14) In the *MFC AppWizard - Step 4 of 6* screen uncheck 4 boxes. Increase number of files to 10. Click Next.

15) In the *MFC AppWizard - Step 5 of 6* screen click Next.

16) In the *MFC AppWizard - Step 6 of 6* screen click Finish.

17) In the *New Project Information* dialog box click *OK* to enter the *ManyDoc* workspace.

You are done - the *ManyDoc* workspace has been created on screen. In the left pane you can examine the project classes, resources, and files. ^{Go} to Section 1.4. When you are done *Click File*, click *Close Workspace*.

1.3 Dialog based

Do Single document/view steps 1 and 2 to create project *Dialog*.

21) In the *MFC AppWizard - Step 1* screen – select *Dialog based*, select your language. Click Next.

22) In the *MFC AppWizard - Step 2 of 4* screen uncheck 3 boxes. You can type the title of the dialog or accept what is written. Click Next.

23) In the *MFC AppWizard - Step 3 of 4* screen click Next.

24) In the *MFC AppWizard – Step4 of 4* screen click Finish.

25) In the *New Project Information* dialog box click *OK* to enter the *Dialog* workspace.

You are done - the *Dialog* workspace has been created on screen. In the left pane you can examine the project classes, resources, and files. When you are done *Click File*, click *Close Workspace*.

1.4 Build and Execute a project

Building a project is straightforward. Build to verify that the project workspace is error free. Watch the build progress in the output pane

To build the project click on *Build menu*.
Click on *Set Active Configuration*
   In the *Set Active Configuration* dialog box click on
   Project-name - Win32Release, click on OK.
Then
Click on *Build menu*.
Click on *Build Project-name.exe*. Watch the output pane. You should see
OneDoc.exe - 0 error(s), 0 warning(s).
Click on *Execute Project-name.exe*
Project-name Window appears. The window is empty. The window title is "Untitled – OneDoc."

> **Later - After adding code to any project file repeat Build a Project to check for errors.**

Examine the files: At the bottom of the left hand panel on the screen click on FileView. In FileView click on all titles until all file names are exposed. Click on a file name. Examine the file contents in the right hand screen panel.

Important: execute a program after a build to make sure it works.

A quick way to open any workspace
For example open the *OneDoc* workspace folder in the Project X folder. Click *OneDoc.dsw*. Right click on *OneDoc.dsw*. Click on *Open with MSDEV*. This action opens Visual C++ and the *OneDoc* workspace.

Where is the dot exe file?
Open the workspace folder. Dot exe is in the release folder.

What do we need to do to make a project program portable (run on any computer)?

For example open the *OneDoc* workspace. Click on *Projects* in the toolbar, click on *Settings* to open the *Project Settings* dialog box. Click on the *C/C++* tab. In the Project Options edit box scroll down to see */Fo"Release/" /Fd"Release/" /FD /c*. If you see other words change to */Fo"Release/" /Fd"Release/" /FD /c*. Click on OK. Build *OneDoc* to make it portable.

1.5 Writing the Window's Title

Writing your title in a window title bar is simply a matter of modifying a string. Open the *OneDoc* workspace.

In the *ResourceView* pane click on OneDoc resources, click on String Table, click on string table.

In the right hand pane click on the IDR_MAINFRAME string. Right click on the string and select properties. Change the strings' **bold type** as shown below. Simply exchange **OneDoc** and **\n.**

From
OneDoc\n\n OneDoc\n\n\nOneDoc.Document\nOneDoc Document
To
\nOneDoc\n OneDoc\n\n\nOneDoc.Document\nOneDoc Document

Build the project, the execute it. The window title is now OneDoc.

If you do not like what has been done in a project you can delete it. Exit Visual C++ 6.0. Go to the Project X folder. Delete the project folder.

2 Hello World Program Design

The traditional "first program" writes the message "Hello World" in a window.

Open Visual C++. Create a single document workspace with name *HelloWorld* (Chapter 1, Section 1.1). Click on *FileView* in the left pane. Click on the source file *HelloWorldView.cpp*. The contents of *HelloWorldView.cpp* appear on the screen.

Since everything in the client window is *drawn* we look for a text drawing function to add to *OnDraw*. We find *TextOut* in the Drawing Text section [JP67].

To understand *TextOut* we now become involved with an incredible amount of detail, which is characteristic of MFC. This is why our focus is limited to functions we had to find and use.

We need the definition of *TextOut*, which we find in the MFC library by typing *TextOut* anywhere on the screen, putting the cursor over it, and pressing F1. Here is most of what appears. Erase *TextOut* when done.

BOOL TextOut(int *x*, int *y*, const CString& *str*);

Return Value Nonzero if the function is successful; otherwise 0.

Parameters
x   Specifies the logical x-coordinate of the starting point of the text.
y   Specifies the logical y-coordinate of the starting point of the text.
str   A **CString** object that contains the characters to be drawn.

Remarks
Writes a character string at the specified location using the currently selected font. Character origins are at the upper-left corner of the character cell. By default, the current position is not used or updated by the function. If an application needs to update the current position when it calls **TextOut**, the application can call the **SetTextAlign** member function with *nFlags* set to **TA_UPDATECP**. When this flag is set, Windows ignores the *x* and *y* parameters on subsequent calls to **TextOut**, using the current position instead.

The parameter *str* is written as *_T ("Hello World")*. The MFC *_T* macro [JP32] used here makes a program indifferent to character set differences. The macro is used as *_T (string in quotes)*.

The *pDC –> TextOut* line is the only code line added to *OnDraw* in *Hello WorldView.cpp*. The arrow operator is used to call *TextOut*, because the *OnDraw* argument *pDC* is a pointer.

```
void CHelloWorldView::OnDraw(CDC* pDC)
{
    CHelloWorldDoc* pDoc = GetDocument();
    ASSERT_VALID(pDoc);
    // TODO: add draw code for native data here
    pDC –> TextOut (200, 200,"Hello World");
}
```

Click on *Build*. (Chapter 1, Section 1.4).
Click on *Build HelloWorld.exe*.
Click on *Execute HelloWorld.exe*

Take a look.

Change 200, 200 to any other x, y coordinates to move the text in the window.

IMPORTANT: Visual C++ simplifies finding information via the F1 key. For example, anywhere in the Visual C++ right hand screen, type any word, highlight it, and press F1. If the word is not legal it simply appears in the index edit box. If the word is legal the MSDN library Topics Found dialog box appears. Click on the line in the box that selects the Microsoft Foundation Class library function.

3 Drawing in a Window

Windows graphics programming was simplified when the *CDC* Graphics Device Interface (GDI) appeared [JP38], because the GDI is a device independent graphics interface. Furthermore MFC adds MFC classes and functions that enhance and work with the GDI [JP38].

Create a single document workspace with name *Drawing*. (Chapter 1, Section 1.1). Click on *FileView* in the left pane. Click on the source file *DrawingView.cpp*. The contents of *DrawingView.cpp* appear on the screen. After adding code later on build the program (Ch 1, Section 1.4).

Device context Windows drawing functions draw in the device context's logical display surface instead of screen pixels. This is how the GDI uses the device context idea [JP38] to ensure that every program draws in its own window, and does not interfere with any other program window,

Before a Windows program can draw any pixels on the screen it must acquire a device context handle from the GDI before being able to draw. For example in *OnDraw(CDC* pDC)* use the following code.

```
CDC* pDC = GetDC ();          // Get Device Context [JP39]
// Draw using pDC -> object
ReleaseDC (pDC);
```

There are four MFC Device Context Classes for *OnPaint( )* [JP39].

Class Name	Description
CPaintDC	For drawing in a window's client area
CClientDC	For drawing in a window's client area
CWindowDC	For drawing anywhere in a window
CMetaFileDC	For drawing to a GDI metafile

Using a device context is straightforward in *OnPaint( )*.

```
CPaintDC dc (this);       // [JP40]
// select desired pen, brush, font
// Draw using  dc.object format
```

```
dc.SetBkMode (TRANSPARENT);     // Text background color is ignored
```

Objects that Draw The classes *CPen*, *CBrush*, and *CFont*. Define pens, brushes, and fonts [JP 60, 64].

The default pen draws solid black lines 1 pixel wide. The default brush paints solid white. The default font is a proportional font with a 12 point height.

```
// Here is how to create your pen [JP60].
```
CPen *name* (**int** *nPenStyle*, **int** *nWidth*, **COLORREF** *crColor*);
```
// For example  create a CPen object
CPen myredpen (PS_SOLID, 4, RGB (255, 0, 0) ;
// or
```
BOOL CreatePen (**int** *nPenStyle*, **int** *nWidth*, **COLORREF** *crColor*);
```
// For example
CPen  mybluepen;          // create a CPen object
mybluepen.CreatPen (PS_SOLID, 10, RGB(0, 0, 255);    //use the dot operator
```

```
// Brushes can be solid, hatched, or patterned.
// Here is how to create your solid brush [JP64].
```
CBrush *name* (**COLORREF** *crColor*);
```
// For example
CBrush yellow_brush (RGB(255,255,100));
```

BOOL CreateSolidBrush (COLORREF *crColor*);
```
//  For example
CBrush yellow_brush;          // create a CBrush object
yellow_brush.CreateSolidBrush (RGB(255,255,100));
```

```
//Here is how to create your hatched brush [JP65].
```
CBrush *name* (int *nIndex*, **COLORREF** *crColor*);
```
CBrush blue_brush (HS_CROSS, RGB (0, 0, 255));
```
 /* **Parameters**
 nIndex Specifies the hatch style of the brush. It can be any one of several styles [JP65]
 crColor Specifies the foreground color of the brush as an RGB color. If the brush is hatched, this parameter specifies the color of the hatching.   */

Changing an Object The *CDC* function used to select a predefined GDI object into a device context is *CDC::SelectObject*. *SelectObject* selects predefined Pens, Brushes, Fonts, Bitmaps, and other objects into a device context [JP73]. Emphasis: Until *SelectObject* is used to change the current pen, brush, or font, the GDI uses the device context's defaults.

Add this sample of drawing code to OnDraw in DrawingView.cpp

```
void CDrawingView::OnDraw(CDC* pDC)
{
    CDrawingDoc* pDoc = GetDocument();
    ASSERT_VALID(pDoc);
    // Draw using pDC -> object
    pDC = GetDC ();          // Get Device Context

    // TODO: Add your message handler code here
    //Pen functions
    pDC -> SetMapMode (MM_LOENGLISH);
    pDC -> MoveTo (100,-20);
    pDC -> LineTo (500, -20);

    CPen redpen (PS_SOLID,4,RGB(255,0,0));
    CPen* pOldPen = pDC -> SelectObject (&redpen);
    pDC -> LineTo (100,-60);

    CPen bluepen (PS_SOLID,10,RGB(0,0,255));
    CPen* pOldPen1 = pDC -> SelectObject (&bluepen);
    pDC -> LineTo (500,-60);

    pDC -> SelectObject (pOldPen);
    pDC -> MoveTo (100,-100);
    pDC -> LineTo (500,-100);
    //Brush functions
    CBrush blue_brush(HS_CROSS, RGB(0,0,255));
    pDC -> SelectObject (&blue_brush);
    CPen* pOldPen2 = pDC -> SelectObject (&redpen);
    pDC -> Rectangle (100, -80, 500, -140);
    CBrush yellow_brush(RGB(255,255,100));
    pDC -> SelectObject (&yellow_brush);
    CPen* pOldPen3 = pDC -> SelectObject (&redpen);
    CRect rect(100, -180, 500, -240);

    pDC -> Rectangle (100, -180, 500, -240);
    pDC -> SetBkMode (TRANSPARENT);
    pDC -> DrawText (_T ("Write in a box"),-1, &rect, DT_SINGLELINE |
                              DT_CENTER | DT_VCENTER);
    pDC -> Ellipse (100, -260, 500, -320);
    pDC -> RoundRect (100, -360, 500, -420, 20, 20);
    ReleaseDC (pDC);
}
```

4 Signal Generator Front Panel Project

A Signal Generator Design project is a working design with three parts: 1) the Signal Generator front panel on the PC screen, 2) the Universal Serial Bus channel, and 3) the Signal Generator hardware that produces signals defined by the front panel via the USB bus. What follows is only about the Signal Generator front panel on the PC screen, because this is about how to program a *dialog based* project using Visual C++.

Knowing that everything on the front panel *has to be drawn* is the key to understanding how a front panel is created.

After opening a *dialog based* project workspace the *front panel* is created in the form of a dialog box *as a main window* [JP432], which is resized to the design size. Then control push buttons and radio buttons are added at locations established by the design. Text boxes showing the current numbers for parameters are added next to associated control buttons. Text labels identify groups of control functions.

The event driven Windows programming model means that clicking on a control is an event that sends a message that calls a message handler function that implements the control's purpose. This capability is implemented by adding MFC skeleton code for event driven message passing. At this point the message handler functions are empty. Each message handler function is then written in MFC code according to the needs of the design. Finally required functions are written to support the message handlers. This completes the front panel design.

The design works as follows. First you *Enter a Number* (Figure 401). The number is entered via the 0 to 9 keypad. If the number is intended to be the *Begin* frequency of a sweep, then you click the *Begin* push button.

Pressing any push button such as *Begin* produces two actions.
1) The number is stored in a register and displayed on the front panel.
2) The number is sent, via the USB bus, to program the hardware.

After all parameters required to program the Signal Generator have been entered press *Start* to produce the signal. Press *Stop* when you are done.

4.1 Create a dialog based project workspace.

Follow the procedure in Chapter 1, Section 1.3 Dialog Based except as follows.

    Type the name *SignalGen* in the *Project Name* edit box.

    Note addition of *SignalGen* in the *Location* edit box.

    In step 2 of 4 screen type the title *Signal Generator 1Hz to 50MHz*

4.2 Build the *SignalGen* Project

Follow the procedure in Chapter 1, Section 1.4.

4.3 Change Dialog size and delete controls

Click on *File*, click on *Open* to get the *Open* dialog box
Change contents of the *Open as* edit box to *Text*
Click on *SignalGen.rc*
Click on Open to open the *dot rc* file
Go to the file's *Dialog* section, and change from
IDD_SIGNALGEN_DIALOG DIALOGEX 0, 0, 320, 200
to
IDD_SIGNALGEN_DIALOG DIALOGEX 0, 0, 675, 200

Click on File, click on *Save as* to get *Save as* dialog box, click on *Save*.
Close the *SignalGen.rc* file.

Click *ResourceView* at bottom of left pane.
Click on +SignalGen Resources.
Click on +Dialog.
Click on IDD_SIGNALGEN_DIALOG.
Observe the new size of the dialog box (the front panel to be).

Click on the *OK* button. Right click, select cut to remove button
Click on the *Cancel* button. Right click, select cut to remove button
Click on *text*. Right click, select cut to remove the text.

> *Emphasis: The dialog box is the front panel*

Figure 401 Signal Generator Front Panel Design

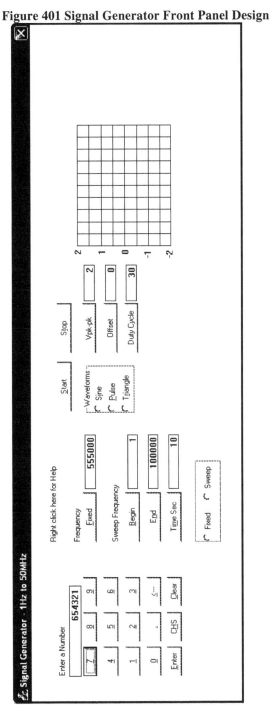

4.4 How to Position a Control

Positioning is *complicated* in Visual C++ 6.0.

To display the front panel click *ResourceView*, *+SignalGen* Resources, +Dialog, and IDD_SIGNALGEN_DIALOG.

There is a status bar directly below the Front Panel. Click on the square of dots (Toggle Grid) next to the right end of the status bar. A dot grid appears on the front panel. Click again and the dots disappear.

Next, click on the funny square (Toggle Guides) at the right end to toggle between *Rulers & Guides* and a plain panel display. When in the plain panel display, click Toggle Grid to add the grid to the display.

You can achieve the same results of you click on *Layout* in the tool bar, and then *Guide Settings*. Do not change the *Guide Settings*.

When in the *Rulers & Guides* display, place the cursor on a ruler and click. Observe that an arrow and a gridline appear. Put the cursor over the arrow, or the gridline, and a <−□> □symbol appears. Press the left mouse button, observe that dimensions appear, and note that a grid line has been added to the display. The arrows and grid lines allow exact positioning.

>>> The arrow keys on the keyboard move selected objects, such as buttons, in small increments.

For example do this: on the x axis place the cursor at coordinates 25, 60, and 95 to get gridlines at coordinates 25, 60, and 95. Repeat for the y axis at coordinates 50, 70, 90, 110, and 130 (Figure 404).

Create the keypad by adding 15 buttons that are aligned with the gridlines (Section 4.5).

Retain the gridlines forever. They simplify the positioning task.

Figure 404 Signal Generator Control Grid

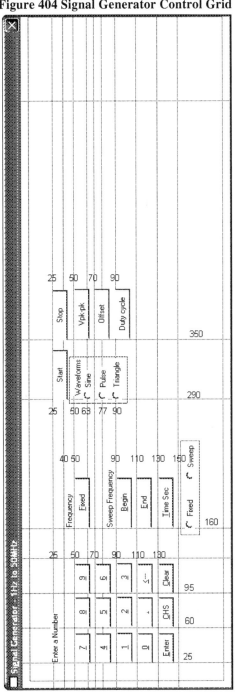

4.5 Keypad and Code for Programming a Number

The purpose here is to add a keypad to the front panel, and the required code that makes the keypad functional; to activate it.

Each key in the 15 key keypad and the associated code is added to the front panel by the following process, which is shown by example as follows.

The example adds one push button, digit 7, to the front panel, and the required code that activates the button.

Emphasis: The finished design works as follows.
1) *Enter a Number* (Figure 401). The number, 1, such as the 72Hz *Begin* frequency of a sweep, is entered via the 0 to 9 keypad.

2) The number creating process ends when *Enter* is pressed.

3) Pressing any push button such as *Begin* produces two actions.
    3.1) The number 72 is stored in the *Begin* register and displayed on the front panel next to the *Begin* push button (Figure 401).
    3.2) The number 72 is sent, via the USB bus, to program the hardware.

4) After all parameters have been entered press *Start* to emit the periodic signal you programmed. Press *Stop* when you are done.

4.5.1 Add a Push Button, Position it, Change Properties
To display the front panel click *ResourceView*, *+SignalGen Resources*, +Dialog, and IDD_SIGNALGEN_DIALOG.

Display the *Front Panel* (Figure 401).
Click on left pane *ResourceView* tab. Click on *+SignalGen Resources* Click on +Dialog. Click on IDD_SIGNALGEN_DIALOG to see the "*Signal Generator 1Hz to 50MHz*" front panel in the right hand pane.

Somewhere on the front panel is a box, the control tool box, containing symbols for the available controls [JP315]. To find out what control a symbol represents let the cursor hover over the symbol for a short time. A ToolTip will appear showing the name of the control associated with the symbol.

Add a control - push button example [JP319]
  Drag a push button from the control tool box onto the front panel
  Position the button[1] at coordinates x=25, y=50 (Figure 404).
  Reduce button width to 30 units. Right click on the button.
  Click on *Properties.*

Figure 402

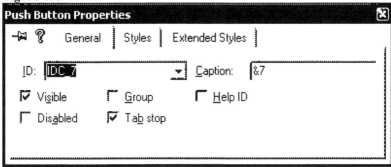

In the Push Button Properties dialog box (Figure 402) click on the
General tab. There are 2 edit boxes *ID* and *Caption*, and 5 check boxes.
        In the *Caption* edit box type *&7.*
        In the *ID* edit box erase *IDC_BUTTON.* Type *IDC_7.*
        Only the check boxes *Visible* and *Tab stop* should be checked.
        Click on the X to close the *Push Button Properties* box.

Add a control – static text example – label the keypad [JP331]
  Drag a static text from the control tool box onto the front panel
  Position the static text at coordinates x=25, y=25 (Figure 404).
  Right click on the button.
  Click on *Properties.*

Click on the *General* tab.
        In the *Caption* edit box type *Enter a Number.*
        In the *ID* edit box change nothing.
        Only the boxes *Visible* and *Group* should be checked.
        Click on the X to close the *Text Properties* box.

---

[1] 4.4 Position a Control page 14

17

4.5.2 Add Push Button Functions for Message Passing

Click on View, click on Class Wizard, click on Message Maps [JP319].

Figure 403 Shows that many buttons have been added to the front panel

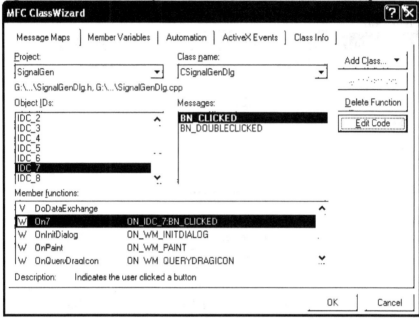

Verify Project is *SignalGen*, Class name is *CSignalGenDlg* (Figure 403).
In the *Object IDs* box click on push button object id *IDC_7*.
In the *Messages* box click *BN_CLICKED*.
The *Add Function* button is activated.
Click on *Add Function* to get *Add Member function* box. Accept *Member function* name *On7*. Click on OK. This adds code items 1, 2, 3.

1) to *SignalGenDlg.h* a prototype function *afx_msg void On7();*

2) to the message map in *SignalGenDlg.cpp* the function
ON_BN_CLICKED(IDC_7, On7)

3) in *SignalGenDlg.cpp* a skeleton message handler
void CSignalGenDlg::On7()

After the 15 keys are programmed the message map in *SignalGenDlg.cpp* includes the following functions. Also see prototypes in file *SignalGenDlg.h* and message handlers in file *SignalGenDlg.cpp*.

```
ON_BN_CLICKED(IDC_0, On0)
ON_BN_CLICKED(IDC_1, On1)
ON_BN_CLICKED(IDC_2, On2)
ON_BN_CLICKED(IDC_3, On3)
ON_BN_CLICKED(IDC_4, On4)
ON_BN_CLICKED(IDC_5, On5)
ON_BN_CLICKED(IDC_6, On6)
ON_BN_CLICKED(IDC_7, On7)
ON_BN_CLICKED(IDC_8, On8)
ON_BN_CLICKED(IDC_9, On9)
ON_BN_CLICKED(IDC_ENTER, OnEnter)
ON_BN_CLICKED(IDC_BACKSPACE, OnBackspace)
ON_BN_CLICKED(IDC_CHGSIGN, OnChgsign)
ON_BN_CLICKED(IDC_CLEAR, OnClear)
ON_BN_CLICKED(IDC_DPOINT, OnDpoint)
```

4.5.3 Add Code to Skeleton Push Button Message Handlers

Many numbers are needed to specify a signal to be generated. This is why we set up a typical number entry push button keypad set: *0 to 9, decimal point, backspace, change sign, clear, and enter*. The number entered is displayed in a text box above the keypad. (Figure 401).

Initially the number is stored as a *string* of characters in *m_strNumber*. The string is converted to a real number by *atof(string)* prior to storage in a number register.

Variable	Reason why it is included
MAXDIGITS 8	A define. It is always prudent to limit number size.
m_iNumDigits	*MAXDIGITS* requires counting digits.
m_bPosNumber	Since sign can be changed by toggling the button *CHS* the current sign is saved.
m_bDecPt	Decimal point status also has to be saved.
m_strNumber	A CString variable storing the number. Each time we click on a 0 to 9 PB the corresponding digit ASCII code is added to a string. See (char) 0x37 code 401.
m_iNumDigits	Add 1 when digit count is incremented.
int *m_iLength*	Adding 0 to 9, period, and sign char change length.
m_bNew	Can enter a new number
m_char	Stores a keypad ASCII character
m_bDecPt	Decimal point is in the number
m_bEnable	Can store the number in any register now

In file *SignalGenDlg.cpp* the message handler *CSignalGenDlg::On7( )* is a skeleton to which code is added to implement the action required when PB 7 is pressed. The same code is used for push buttons 0 to 9.

Action - add *#define MAXDIGITS 8* to *SignalGenDlg.cpp*
Action - add variables to *SignalGenDlg.h*
  BOOL m_bNew;   *int m_iNumDigits;*   *CString m_strNumber;*
Action - add *Number buttons* Code 401 to *SignalGenDlg.cpp*.

Code 401 Number buttons 0 to 9

```
void CSignalGenDlg::On7()     // the following executes when PB 7 is pressed.
{
    if (m_iNumDigits == MAXDIGITS) {
       AfxMessageBox ("8 digits maximum", MB_OK); // message to output
    }
    else {
       if (m_bNew) {                    // OK to enter a new number
          m_strNumber += (char) 0x37;   // add ASCII char for digit 7 to string
          m_iNumDigits++;               // add 1
          Invalidate (FALSE);           // repaint the window
       }
    }
}
```

MAXDIGITS When building a number via a keypad the number of digits in the number needs to be limited for practical reasons. The 50MHz upper limit is why *MAXDIGITS* is defined as 8. *MAXDIGITS* is a symbolic constant defined by a #define line of code. For example:

#define name   *replacement text*
#define MAXDIGITS   *8*

To show the advantage of defines, suppose 8 is used 122 times in the code. Then a change to 10 would require 122 changes of 8 to 10.

On the other hand if *MAXDIGITS* is used 122 times only ONE change of 8 to 10 implements 122 changes when the *MAXDIGITS* is changed from 8 to 10.

A *body* of code is bound by two brackets as in { ... }.

If–else statement is written as follows:
if (condition)
{
    If the condition is true execute the statements in this body.
}
else
{
    If the condition is false execute the statements in this body.
}

If–else condition The condition is *m_iNumDigits == MAXDIGITS*.
In C languages == is the "equals" operator, whereas = is the assignment operator. The condition is true when variable *m_iNumDigits* has value 8, which equals MAXDIGITS.

The variable is defined as an integer as follows: *int m_iNumDigits;*

If the current key press of 7 means this 7 is the 8th digit, then when the 7 is stored (by the else statement) *m_iNumDigits* is increased to 8. Any additional digit 0 to 9 will not be stored, because now *m_iNumDigits* = 8 = *MAXDIGITS*.

Condition-is-true Then the *if* body emits a message that warns the user.
   AfxMessageBox ("8 digits maximum", MB_OK); // message to output

Condition-is-false Then the *else* body processes the digits.
  if (m_bNew) {   // OK to enter a new number
    m_strNumber += (char) 0x37; // add ASCII char for digit 7 to string
    m_iNumDigits++;   // add 1 to count digits
    Invalidate (FALSE);   // repaint the window
  }

Message handler *On(7)* stores the 7 digit as a character in a string of characters *m_strNumber* (an MFC *CString* data type). Digit 7 is stored as a character, because 0x37 is the ASCII[6] code binary word a keyboard emits when key 7 is pressed. The hidden logic here is the code a keyboard produces. Knowing how to program requires knowing the code devices produce.

---

[6] ASCII - American Standard Code for Information Interchange

Programming with MFC

Action – add *BOOL m_bDecPt*, and *int m_iLength* to *SignalGenDlg.h.*
Action - add *Decimal Point* Code 402 to *SignalGenDlg.cpp.*

Code 402 Decimal Point

```
void CSignalGenDlg::OnDpoint()
{
    if (m_bDecPt == TRUE) {return ;}    // exit if decimal point is in the number
    m_iLength = m_strNumber.GetLength ();        // get string length
    if (m_iLength == MAXDIGITS) {
      // if max digits do not add any more chars
      AfxMessageBox ("8 digits maximum", MB_OK); // message to output
    }
    else {
        if (m_bNew) {                        // OK to add decimal point
        m_strNumber += (char) 0x2E;    // ASCII code for decimal point [JP444]
        m_bDecPt = TRUE;                // decimal point now in number
        Invalidate (FALSE);              // repaint the window
        }
    }
}
```

Click the keypad *decimal point* button to execute OnDpoint( ). This function is similar to On7( ) where 0x2E (ASCII code for decimal point) replaces 0x37 (ASCII code for 7) and two statements are added.

1) if (m_bDecPt == TRUE) {return;}   // exit if a decimal point is in the number.
A true condition executes *return*, which forces an exit from OnDpoint( ), because only one decimal point is allowed in a number.
Declare as *BOOL m_bDecPt;*

2) m_iLength = m_strNumber.GetLength ();   // get string length
int m_iLength;
Use *CString::GetLength* // an MFC member of the CString class.

CString object *m_strNumber* can use the dot operator to use the CString member function *GetLength* or any other member function. To discover CString member functions place the Visual C++ cursor over the word CString and press F1.

22

Action – add variable *Char m_char* to *SignalGenDlg.h*
Action - add *Backspace* Code 403 to *SignalGenDlg.cpp*

Code 403 Backspace

```
// If backspace removes a digit or decimal point, then m_iNumDigits – 1.
// If backspace removes the decimal point then m_bDecPt = FALSE
void CSignalGenDlg::OnBackspace ()
{
    if (m_bNew) {
        int m_iLength = m_strNumber.GetLength ();   // use GetLength function
        m_char = m_strNumber [m_iLength  – 1];      // fetch next char

    if (m_iLength != 0) {
            if (m_char != _T('.'))  {
                m_iNumDigits —;
            }
            else {
                m_bDecPt = FALSE;
            }

            m_strNumber = m_strNumber.Left (m_iLength – 1);
            // extracts leftmost m_iLengt h – 1 chars to store
            Invalidate (FALSE);                     // repaint the window
        }
    }
}
```

If *m_bNew* is true we can add digits to, or delete digits from, the number we are building. *GetLength( )* is an MFC CString member function. Use the dot operator to call this member function to get a count of the bytes in this **CString** object. The count does not include a null terminator.

Bytes in a string are numbered from 0, so the last char is at position m_iLength – 1 (7 bytes in the string of length 7 are numbered 0 to 6).

Declare as *char m_char;*

If the string length is > 0, and if the last char is NOT a dp, then it is a digit that will be removed. So decrease m_iNumDigits by 1. Else the last char is a dp that will be removed. So set m_bDecPt to FALSE. The last char is removed indirectly by rewriting the string with the first m_iLength – 2 chars. Here is the MFC function that does that.
    m_strNumber = m_strNumber.Left (m_iLength – 1);

Action – add 3 variables to *SignalGenDlg.h*
  BOOL m_bEnable;   BOOL m_bPosNumber;   double m_dNumber
Action - add *OnEnter* Code 404 to *SignalGenDlg.cpp*

Code 404 Enter

```
void CSignalGenDlg::OnEnter()
{
    m_bEnable = TRUE;            // can store number in any register now
    m_bNew = FALSE;             // cannot build a new number now
    m_iNumDigits = 0;           // prepare for new number
    m_bPosNumber = TRUE;        // ready for new number
    m_bDecPt = FALSE;           // ready for new number
    m_dNumber = atof(m_strNumber);
    // convert number string to floating point double number
    Invalidate (FALSE);
}
```

Action - add *OnChgsgn* Code 405 to *SignalGenDlg.cpp*

Code 405 Change Sign to *SignalGenDlg.cpp*

```
void CSignalGenDlg::OnChgsgn()
{
    if (m_bNew) {
        if (m_bPosNumber == TRUE) {            // if positive do this [JP443]
            m_strNumber = _T ("–") + m_strNumber; // add minus sign to string
            m_bPosNumber = FALSE;              // number is now negative
        }
        else {                                 // number is negative
            m_iLength = m_strNumber.GetLength (); // use GetLength()
            if (m_iLength != 0) {
            m_strNumber = m_strNumber.Right (m_iLength – 1);
            // delete minus sign by fetching rightmost m_iLength 1 chars
            }
            m_bPosNumber = TRUE;               // number is now positive
        }
        Invalidate (FALSE);                    // repaint the window
    }
}
```

Action - add *Unclear* Code 406 to *SignalGenDlg.cpp*

Code 406 Clear

```
void CSignalGenDlg::OnClear()
{
  m_bNew = TRUE;              //enable storing digits into Number register
  m_iNumDigits = 0;          // ready for new number
  m_bPosNumber = TRUE;       // start with positive number
  m_bDecPt = FALSE;          // start with no decimal point
  m_bEnable = FALSE;         // disable storing a num in any register
  m_strNumber.Empty ();      // empty the number string
  Invalidate (FALSE);        // repaint the window
}
```

4.5.4 Add Push Button Member Variables

The message handler code for the 15 keypad buttons requires variables listed in 4.5.3 page 19.

Action–add Code 407 to *CSignalGenDlg::CSignalGenDlg* after *m_hIcon* in *SignalGenDlg.cpp*.

Code 407

```
// init variables   KEYPAD
m_bDecPt = FALSE;        // start with no decimal point
m_bEnable = FALSE;       // disable storing digits into any register
m_bNew = TRUE;           // enable storing digits into Number register
m_bPosNumber = TRUE;     // start with positive number

m_iLength = 0;           // start with no char in string
m_iNumDigits = 0;        // start with empty string
m_strNumber = _T("654321");
```

4.5.5 Add *OnPaint* Code

Find *OnPaint*: A straightforward way to find *OnPaint* is to click on *ClassView* in the Visual C++ left pane. Then click on *+CSignalGenDlg* to see all functions. Find *OnPaint* in the list and click on it.

WaveformScreen function (page 41) paints the waveform screen on the front panel. Pressing a waveform button (sine, pulse, triangle) erases any waveform on the screen, and paints the selected waveform (sine, pulse, triangle) on the waveform screen.

Numbers are placed in text boxes. A brush specifies the text box color. The font is the device context default font.

Text box coordinates are specified. They are used to define a device context rectangle. *Rectangle* and *TextOut* are MFC functions.

Add Code 408 to OnPaint in *SignalGenDlg.cpp*. Delete *if (IsIconic)*.

Code 408 Code to add to OnPaint

```
void CSignalGenDlg::OnPaint()
{
    CPaintDC dc(this);                      // device context for painting
    // select rectangles' body brush color
    CBrush brush (RGB (255, 255, 213));         // [JP64]
    CBrush* pOldBrush = dc.SelectObject (&brush);   // [JP43]
    // Initialize the device context.
    dc.SetTextAlign (TA_RIGHT | TA_BOTTOM);     // [JP67]
    dc.SetBkMode (TRANSPARENT);                 // [JP43]
    // keypad
    int x1 = 37, dx1 = 80;
    int y1 = 60, dy1 = 17, dy11 = 16;
    dc.Rectangle (x1, y1, x1+dx1, y1+dy1);     // the body of the Number display
    dc.TextOut (x1+dx1, y1+dy11, m_strNumber);  // print the Number
}
```

4.6 Code for Programming a Frequency

Add controls to the front panel that program the signal generator frequency: push buttons, *Fixed*, *Begin*, *End*, and *Time Sec*, radio buttons *Fixed*, and *Sweep* , and static texts *Frequency* and *Sweep Frequency* (Figure 404, page 15).

To add buttons copy the process in Sections 4.5.1 and 4.5.2 page 16.

Button program additions
1) 6 buttons to the front panel

2) 6 prototypes to *SignalGenDlg.h*
  afx_msg void OnBegin();
  afx_msg void OnEnd();
  afx_msg void OnFixed();
  afx_msg void OnRfixed();
  afx_msg void OnRsweep();
  afx_msg void OnTimesec();

3) 6 functions to the message map in *SignalGenDlg.cpp*.
  ON_BN_CLICKED(IDC_FIXED, OnFixed)
  ON_BN_CLICKED(IDC_BEGIN, OnBegin)
  ON_BN_CLICKED(IDC_END, OnEnd)
  ON_BN_CLICKED(IDC_TIMESEC, OnTimesec)
  ON_BN_CLICKED(IDC_RSWEEP, OnRsweep)   radio button
  ON_BN_CLICKED(IDC_RFIXED, OnRfixed)   radio button

4) 6 functions to *SignalGenDlg.cpp*
  OnFixed, OnBegin, OnEnd, OnTimeSec, OnRsweep, OnRFixed

How it works: Click on the *Fixed* radio button. Use the keypad to create the fixed frequency number. After *Enter* is pressed, press the *Fixed* PB to store the number in the *Fixed* frequency register.

If a signal whose frequency is to be swept over a range of frequencies click on the *Sweep* radio button. Then the beginning and end frequency numbers are created via the keypad and stored in the *Begin* and *End* frequency registers.

Create, via the keypad, the beginning to end sweep time number. Store it in the *Time sec* register.

Programming with MFC

Action – add 2 variables to *SignalGenDlg.h*
   double m_dFixed   CString m_strFixed
Action - add *Fixed Frequency* Code 409 to *SignalGenDlg.cpp*

Code 409 Fixed Frequency

```
void CSignalGenDlg::OnFixed()
{
  if (m_bEnable) {
    m_strFixed = m_strNumber;              // transfer number to Fixed
    m_strNumber.Empty ();                  // erase the number in the string
    m_dFixed = atof(m_strFixed);   // convert number to a floating point double

    if (m_dFixed < 0) {              // if the number is negative make it positive
       m_iLength = m_strFixed.GetLength ();
         if (m_iLength != 0) {
         m_strFixed = m_strFixed.Right (m_iLength – 1);       // extracts chars
         }
    }

    m_dFixed = atof(m_strFixed);      // convert string to f point double number

    if (m_dFixed < 1) {                          // if the number is <1 make it = 1.
      m_strFixed = _T("1");
      m_dFixed = atof(m_strFixed);
    }
  }

// add code here that sends m_iNumber to siggen device via USB channel.
    m_bEnable = FALSE;                        // disable programming
    m_bNew = TRUE;                            // enable entering a new number
    Invalidate (FALSE);                       // repaint the window
}
```

Action – add 2 variables to *SignalGenDlg.h*
   double m_dBegin   CString m_strBegin
Action - add *Begin Frequency* Code 410 to *SignalGenDlg.cpp*

Code 410 Begin Frequency

```
void CSignalGenDlg::OnBegin()
// same as OnFixed by replacing m_strFixed with m_strBegin
// and m_dFixed with m_dBegin.
```

28

Action – add 2 variables to *SignalGenDlg.h*
    double m_dEnd   CString m_strEnd
Action - add *End Frequency* Code 411 to *SignalGenDlg.cpp*

Code 411 End Frequency

```
void CSignalGenDlg::OnEnd()
// same as OnFixed by replacing m_strFixed with m_strEnd
// and m_dFixed with m_dEnd.
```

Action – add 2 variables to *SignalGenDlg.h*
    double m_dTsec   CString m_strTsec
Action - add *Time Sec* Code 412 to *SignalGenDlg.cpp*

Code 412 Time Sec

```
// add   #include "math.h" to SignalGenDlg.cpp
void CSignalGenDlg::OnTimesec()
{
    if (m_bEnable) {
        m_strTsec = m_strNumber;        // transfer number to time sec
        m_strNumber.Empty ();           // erase the number
        m_dTsec = atof(m_strTsec);   //convert number to a floating point double

        if (m_dTsec > 50)
        { m_strTsec = _T("50");}            // limit time to 50 seconds

        if (m_dTsec < –50)
        { m_strTsec = _T("50");}            // make time number positive

        m_dTsec = atof(m_strTsec);   //convert number to a floating point double
        if (m_dTsec < 0.0) {                  // remove the minus sign
          m_dTsec = fabs (m_dTsec);       //get absolute value of floating point
          m_iLength = m_strTsec.GetLength ();
          if (m_iLength != 0)
          {m_strTsec = m_strTsec.Right (m_iLength – 1) ;}  // extracts chars
        }
    }
// add code here that sends m_dTsec to siggen device via USB channel.
  m_bEnable = FALSE;
  m_bNew = TRUE;
  Invalidate (FALSE);
}
```

Programming with MFC

Action - add *Rsweep* Code 413 to *SignalGenDlg.cpp*

Code 413 Rsweep

```
void CSignalGenDlg::OnRsweep()
{
  // add code here that sends "SWEEP FREQUENCY" to siggen device via
  // USB channel.
}
```

Action - add Rfixed Code 414 to *SignalGenDlg.cpp*

Code 414 Rfixed

```
void CSignalGenDlg::OnRfixed()
{
  // add code here that sends "FIXED FREQUENCY" to siggen device via
  // USB channel.
}
```

Add a group box around radio buttons *Fixed* & *Sweep* [JP323].

Add *Initialized Variables* Code 415 to *CSignalGenDlg::CSignalGenDlg* in *SignalGenDlg.cpp*

Code 415 Initialized Variables

```
// FREQUENCIES //nlp
  m_dFixed = 555000;
  m_dBegin = 1;
  m_dEnd = 100000;
  m_dTsec = 10;
  m_strFixed = _T("555000");
  m_strBegin = _T("1");
  m_strEnd = _T("100000");
  m_strTsec = _T("10");
```

CString member function *Right (m_iLength − 1)* only copies char to the right of the minus sign effectively deleting it. *m_iLength − 1* is the number of characters to extract from the *m_strFixed* CString object

Add code 416 to *OnPaint* in *SignalGenDlg.cpp* to show the frequency text boxes

Code 416 Add to OnPaint

```
// Frequency
    int x2 = 325, dx2 = 80, y2 = 85, dy2 = 20, dy22 = 18;
    int y3 = 150, dy3 = 20, dy33 = 18;

    // B1-Draw the body of the Fixed display.
    dc.Rectangle (x2, y2, x2+dx2, y2+dy2);
    // B1-print the fixed frequency
    dc.TextOut (x2+dx2–5, y2+dy22, m_strFixed);
    // --------------------
    // B2-Draw the body of the Begin display.
    dc.Rectangle (x2, y3, x2+dx2, y3+dy3);
    // B2-print the begin frequency
    dc.TextOut (x2+dx2–5, y3+dy33, m_strBegin);
    //--------------------
    // B3-Draw the body of the End display.
    dc.Rectangle (x2, y3+32, x2+dx2, y3+32+dy3);
    // B3-print the end frequency
    dc.TextOut (x2+dx2–5, y3+32+dy33, m_strEnd);
    //--------------------
    // B4-Draw the body of the Tsec display.
    dc.Rectangle (x2, y3+64, x2+dx2, y3+64+dy3);
    // B4-print Tsec
    dc.TextOut (x2+dx2–5, y3+64+dy33, m_strTsec);
```

4.7 Code for Programming a Waveform

Add, to the front panel, three radio buttons, *Sine, Pulse, Triangle*, three push buttons *Vpk pk, Offset, Duty Cycle*, and a *Waveforms static box* that program the signal generator amplitude and duty cycle (Figure 404, page 15). Then add *Start* and *Stop* buttons.

To add buttons copy the process in Sections 4.5.1 and 4.5.2 page 16.

Button programming additions
1) 8 buttons to the front panel

2) 8 prototypes to *SignalGenDlg.h*
   afx_msg void OnPulse();
   afx_msg void OnSine();
   afx_msg void OnTriangle();
   afx_msg void OnVpkpk();
   afx_msg void OnOffset();
   afx_msg void OnDutyCycle();
   afx_msg void OnStart();
   afx_msg void OnStop();

3) 8 functions to the message map in *SignalGenDlg.cpp*.
ON_BN_CLICKED(IDC_PULSE, OnPulse)
ON_BN_CLICKED(IDC_SINE, OnSine)
ON_BN_CLICKED(IDC_TRIANGLE, OnTriangle)
ON_BN_CLICKED(IDC_VPKPK, OnVpkpk)
ON_BN_CLICKED(IDC_OFFSET, OnOffset)
ON_BN_CLICKED(IDC_DUTYCYCLE, OnDutyCycle)
ON_BN_CLICKED(IDC_START, OnStart)
ON_BN_CLICKED(IDC_STOP, OnStop)

4) 8 functions to *SignalGenDlg.cpp*
OnPulse, OnSine, OnTriangle, OnVpkpk, OnOffset, OnDutyCycle, ..
OnStart, OnStop

Add a group box around radio buttons, *Sine, Pulse, Triangle* [JP323].

The waveform functions *Sine, Pulse, Triangle* are selected in *OnPaint* by a true *if* condition in each function (page 38). Codes 417, 418, and 419 set the true condition.

Action – add 3 variables to *SignalGenDlg.h*
   BOOL m_bSine;   *BOOL m_bPulse;*   *BOOL m_bTriangle;*
Action - add *OnSine* radio button Code 417 to *SignalGenDlg.cpp*

Code 417 OnSine

```
void CSignalGenDlg::OnSine( )
  {
  m_bSine = 1;          // select sine
  m_bPulse = 0;
  m_bTriangle = 0;
  Invalidate (FALSE);
}
```

Action - add *OnPulse* radio button Code 418 to *SignalGenDlg.cpp*

Code 418 OnPulse

```
void CSignalGenDlg::OnPulse()
{
  m_bSine = 0;
  m_bPulse = 1;         // select pulse
  m_bTriangle = 0;
  Invalidate (FALSE);
}
```

Action - add *OnTriangle* radio button Code 419 to *SignalGenDlg.cpp*

Code 419 OnTriangle

```
void CSignalGenDlg::OnTriangle()
{
  m_bSine = 0;
  m_bPulse = 0;
  m_bTriangle = 1;       // select  triangle
  Invalidate (FALSE);
}
```

Action – add 2 variables to *SignalGenDlg.h*
  double m_dVpp   CString m_strVpp
Action - add *Vpkpk* button Code 420 to *SignalGenDlg.cpp*

Code 420 Vpkpk

```
void CSignalGenDlg::OnVpkpk()
{
    if (m_bEnable) {
      m_strVpp = m_strNumber;
      m_strNumber.Empty ();
      m_dVpp = atof(m_strVpp);

      if (m_dVpp > 2.0)              // peak to peak voltage limit to ± 2 volts max
        { m_strVpp = _T("2");}

      if (m_dVpp < –2.0)
        { m_strVpp = _T("2");}

      m_dVpp = atof(m_strVpp);

      if (m_dVpp < 0.0)  // remove the minus sign
      {
          m_dVpp = fabs(m_dVpp);
          m_iLength = m_strVpp.GetLength ();
          if (m_iLength != 0)
          {m_strVpp = m_strVpp.Right (m_iLength – 1) ;}
      }
      // add code that sends m_dVpp to siggen device via USB channel.
      m_bEnable = FALSE;
      m_bNew = TRUE;
      Invalidate (FALSE);
    }
}
```

Action - add Code 421 and 422 to *SignalGenDlg.cpp*
Code 421

```
void CSignalGenDlg::OnStart()
{ // add code here that sends "Start" to siggen device via USB channel. }
```

Code 422

```
void CSignalGenDlg::OnStop()
{ // add code here that sends "Stop" to siggen device via USB channel. }
```

Action – add 2 variables to *SignalGenDlg.h*
  double m_dOffset   CString m_strOffset
Action - add *Offset* button Code 423 to *SignalGenDlg.cpp*

Code 423 Offset

```
void CSignalGenDlg::OnOffset()
{
    if (m_bEnable) {
      m_strOffset = m_strNumber;
      m_strNumber.Empty ();
      m_dOffset = atof(m_strOffset);

      if (m_dOffset > 1.0)          //  offset limited to –1 volt to +1 volt range
      { m_strOffset = _T("1");}

      if (m_dOffset < –1.0)
      { m_strOffset = _T("−1");}

      m_dOffset = atof(m_strOffset);
      // add code that sends m_dOffset to siggen device via USB channel.
      m_bEnable = FALSE;
      m_bNew = TRUE;
      Invalidate (FALSE);
    }
}
```

Action - add Initialized Variables Code 424 to
CSignalGenDlg::CSignalGenDlg in *SignalGenDlg.cpp*

Code 424 Initialized Variables

```
// WAVEFORMS
  m_dVpp = 2;
  m_dOffset = 0;
  m_dDutyCycle = 30;
  m_strVpp = _T("2");
  m_strOffset = _T("0");
  m_strDutyCycle = _T("30");
  m_bSine = 0;
  m_bPulse = 0;
  m_bTriangle = 0;
```

Programming with MFC

Action – add 2 variables to *SignalGenDlg.h*
    double m_dDutyCycle   CString m_strDutyCycle
Action - add Duty Cycle push button Code 425 to *SignalGenDlg.cpp*

Code 425 Duty Cycle

```
void CSignalGenDlg::OnDutycycle()
{
    if (m_bEnable) {
      m_strDutyCycle = m_strNumber;
      m_strNumber.Empty ();
      m_dDutyCycle = atof(m_strDutyCycle);

      if (m_dDutyCycle > 90)      // duty cycle limited to 10% to 90% range
      { m_strDutyCycle = _T("90");}

      if (m_dDutyCycle < 10)
      { m_strDutyCycle = _T("10");}
      m_dDutyCycle = atof(m_strDutyCycle);
      // add code here that sends m_dDutyCycle to siggen device.
      m_bEnable = FALSE;
      m_bNew = TRUE;
      Invalidate (FALSE);
    }
}
```

Action - add Code 426 to *OnPaint* to show the waveform text boxes.

Code 426 waveforms

```
  int x4 = 610, dx4 = 40, y4 = 85, dy4 = 20, dy44 = 18;
  // C1-Draw the body of the Vpp display.
  dc.Rectangle (x4, y4, x4+dx4, y4+dy4);
  // C1-print Vpp
  dc.TextOut (x4+dx4–5, y4+dy44, m_strVpp);
    // C2-Draw the body of the Offset display.
    dc.Rectangle (x4, y4+32, x4+dx4, y4+32+dy4);
    // C2-print the offset
    dc.TextOut (x4+dx4–5, y4+32+dy44, m_strOffset);
  // C3-Draw the body of the Duty Cycle display.
  dc.Rectangle (x4, y4+64, x4+dx4, y4+64+dy4);
  // C3-print the duty cycle
  dc.TextOut (x4+dx4–5, y4+64+dy44, m_strDutyCycle);
```

4.8 Functions that support the Waveform Display

The front panel waveform display does not program the hardware. The display is a convenience for the user.

All waveforms have 2 volt peak to peak maximum amplitude.

Voltage offset is restricted to ±1 Volt.

Duty cycle is restricted to 10% to 90% range.

Action - add waveform Defines Code 427 to *SignalGenDlg.cpp*
Code 427 Defines

```
#define u0  750      // screen coordinates
#define v0 –80
#define u1 950
#define v1 –240
#define HOUT 10
#define VOUT 8
```

Class Wizard cannot assist with waveform support functions.
Add function prototypes Code 428 by hand to *SignalGenDlg.h*
Code 428 Function Prototypes

```
void WaveformScreen ();
void Sine (BOOL m_bSine, double m_dOffset, double m_dVpp);
void Pulse (BOOL m_bPulse, double m_dOffset, double m_dVpp, double m_dDutyCycle);
void Triangle (BOOL m_bTriangle, double m_dOffset, double m_dVpp);
```

Action - add Code 429 by hand to *OnPaint* in *SignalGenDlg.cpp*. Then comment out Code 429 until the function code is entered.
Code 429 Functions

```
WaveformScreen();
Sine (m_bSine, m_dOffset, m_dVpp);
Pulse (m_bPulse, m_dOffset, m_dVpp, m_dDutyCycle);
Triangle (m_bTriangle, m_dOffset, m_dVpp);
```

Plots are more easily programmed if plots are deviations from zero. Therefore max volts dv=m_Vpp/2   dv=1 max.
And, max volts offset df=-m_dOffset/4 * (v1–v0),
so that max df = −1/4*(−195+35) =40 or 1 volt equivalent

The sine function defines the sine waveform.

Sine[j].x = u0+ (j * (u1–u0) / SEGMENTS) = 600+ (j*200)/10000
so that x ranges from 600 to 800 in 10,000 steps.

Sine[j].y = [df+v0+ (v1–v0)/2] + [dv * (v1–v0)/4 *–sin (4 * PI * j/SEGMENTS)] = [40–35–160/2] + [1*(–160)/4*–sin (4 PI j/10000)]
= –75+40 sin (4 PI j/10000)

where

for two waveforms (4 PI j/10000) ranges from 0 to 4 cycles, and the –75 puts the waveform zero in the vertical center of the output box.

Action - add Sine Code 430 to *SignalGenDlg.cpp*
Code 430 Sine

```
#define SEGMENTS 10000      // waveform constants
#define PI 3.1415926
#define PULSE 9
#define TRIANGLE 5

void CSignalGenDlg::Sine (BOOL m_bSine, double m_dOffset, double m_dVpp)
  // [JP 55]
{
    if (m_bSine == 1)
    {
      CClientDC dc (this);
      dc.SetMapMode (MM_LOENGLISH);
      CPen pen1 (PS_SOLID, 2, RGB (0, 0, 0,));          // [JP 60, 61]
      CPen* pOldPen1 = dc.SelectObject (&pen1);

      double dv = m_dVpp/2;
      double df = -m_dOffset/4 * (v1–v0);
      CPoint Sine[SEGMENTS];

      for (int j=0; j<SEGMENTS; j++)
      {
        Sine[j].x = u0+(j * (u1-u0) / SEGMENTS );
        Sine[j].y = df+v0+ (v1–v0)/2+ dv * (v1–v0)/4 * –sin (4 * PI * j/SEGMENTS);
      }
      dc.Polyline (Sine, SEGMENTS);
    }
    return;
}
```

An array of points defines the pulse waveform. The function *dc.Polyline (Pulse, PULSE)* draws from point to point to produce the waveform.

Action - add Pulse Code 431 to *SignalGenDlg.cpp*
Code 431 Pulse

```
void CSignalGenDlg::Pulse (BOOL m_bPulse, double m_dOffset, double
m_dVpp, double m_dDutyCycle)
{
//duty cycle
  if (m_bPulse == 1)    {
    CClientDC dc (this);
    dc.SetMapMode (MM_LOENGLISH);

    CPen pen1 (PS_SOLID, 2, RGB (0, 0, 0,));  //P 60, 61
    CPen* pOldPen1 = dc.SelectObject (&pen1);
    double dv = m_dVpp/2;
    double df = –m_dOffset/4 * (v1–v0);
    double ddc = m_dDutyCycle/100;
    double dx = (u1–u0)/2;
    double dy = ((v1–v0)/4)*dv;

    CPoint Pulse [PULSE];
    Pulse[0].x = u0;
    Pulse[1].x = u0;
    Pulse[2].x = u0+1*dx*ddc;
    Pulse[3].x = u0+1*dx*ddc;
    Pulse[4].x = u0+1*dx;
    Pulse[5].x = u0+1*dx;
    Pulse[6].x = u0+1*dx+1*dx*ddc;
    Pulse[7].x = u0+1*dx+1*dx*ddc;
    Pulse[8].x = u0+2*dx;
    Pulse [0].y = df+v0+ (v1–v0)/2+dy;
    Pulse [1].y = df+v0+ (v1–v0)/2-dy;
    Pulse [2].y = df+v0+ (v1–v0)/2-dy;
    Pulse [3].y = df+v0+ (v1–v0)/2+dy;
    Pulse [4].y = df+v0+ (v1–v0)/2+dy;
    Pulse [5].y = df+v0+ (v1–v0)/2-dy;
    Pulse [6].y = df+v0+ (v1–v0)/2-dy;
    Pulse [7].y = df+v0+ (v1–v0)/2+dy;
    Pulse [8].y = df+v0+ (v1–v0)/2+dy;
    dc.Polyline (Pulse, PULSE);
  }
  return;
}
```

An array of points defines the triangle waveform. The function *dc.Polyline (Triangle, TRIANGLE)* draws from point to point to produce the waveform.

Action - add Triangle Code 432 to *SignalGenDlg.cpp*
Code 432 Triangle

```
void CSignalGenDlg::Triangle (BOOL m_bTriangle, double m_dOffset, double
m_dVpp)
{
  if (m_bTriangle == 1)
  {
    CClientDC dc (this);
    dc.SetMapMode (MM_LOENGLISH);

    CPen pen1 (PS_SOLID, 2, RGB (0, 0, 0,)); //P 60, 61
    CPen* pOldPen1 = dc.SelectObject (&pen1);
    double dv = m_dVpp/2;
    double df = –m_dOffset/4 * (v1–v0);
    double dx = (u1–u0)/4;
    double dy = ((v1–v0)/4)*dv;

    CPoint Triangle[TRIANGLE];
    Triangle[0].x = u0;
    Triangle[1].x = u0+dx;
    Triangle[2].x = u0+2*dx;
    Triangle[3].x = u0+3*dx;
    Triangle[4].x = u0+4*dx;

    Triangle [0].y = df+v0+ (v1–v0)/2+dy;      //v0+3*dy+df;
    Triangle [1].y = df+v0+ (v1–v0)/2-dy;      //v0+1*dy+df;
    Triangle [2].y = df+v0+ (v1–v0)/2+dy;      //v0+3*dy+df;
    Triangle [3].y = df+v0+ (v1–v0)/2-dy;      //v0+1*dy+df;
    Triangle [4].y = df+v0+ (v1–v0)/2+dy;      //v0+3*dy+df;

    dc.Polyline (Triangle, TRIANGLE);
  }
  return;
}
```

Action - add waveform screen Code 433 in *SignalGenDlg.cpp* Then add *WaveformScreen ()* to *OnPaint*.
Code 433 waveform screen

```
void CSignalGenDlg::WaveformScreen()
{
  CClientDC dc (this);
  dc.SetMapMode (MM_LOENGLISH);
  dc.SetTextAlign (TA_RIGHT | TA_BOTTOM);
  dc.SetBkMode (TRANSPARENT);
  // select body brush color
  CBrush brush (RGB (255, 255, 213));
  CBrush* pOldBrush = dc.SelectObject (&brush);
  // draw output    // create gray solid pen
  CPen pen0 (PS_SOLID, 1, RGB (130, 130, 130,)); //light gray P 60, 61
  CPen* pOldPen0 = dc.SelectObject (&pen0);    //Prosise 60
  // K-Draw the body of the Output display and  print Output
  dc.Rectangle (u0, v0, u1, v1);
  // dc.TextOut (u0+100, v0+2, "Output Voltage");
  // Draw H and V lines
  int dx= (u1– u0)/HOUT;
  int dy= (v1– v0)/VOUT;
  int i;
  // H-Draw the Output horizontal lines.
  for (i=1; i<VOUT; i++) {
    dc.MoveTo(u0, v0+(dy*i));
    dc.LineTo(u1, v0+(dy*i));
  }
  // V-Draw the Output vertical lines.
  for (i=1; i<HOUT; i++) {
    dc.MoveTo(u0+(dx*i), v0);
    dc.LineTo(u0+(dx*i), v1);
  }
  // create black solid pen
  CPen pen1 (PS_SOLID, 1, RGB (0, 0, 0,)); //P 60, 61
  CPen* pOldPen1 = dc.SelectObject (&pen1);
// H-Draw Zero line.
  dc.MoveTo(u0, v0+(dy*4));
  dc.LineTo(u1, v0+(dy*4));
  // draw output voltage scale
  dc.TextOut (u0-5, v0–10, "2");
  dc.TextOut (u0-5, v0–50, "1");
  dc.TextOut (u0-5, v0–90, "0");
  dc.TextOut (u0-6, v0–128, "-1");
  dc.TextOut (u0-6, v0–165, "-2");
  return;
} //end of WaveformScreen
```

4.9 A Simple Help Program

This is the simple help system. A right mouse click accesses it.
Click on *View*, click on *Class Wizard*, click on *Message Maps*.
Check project is *SignalGen*, class name is *CSignalGenDlg*
In the *Object Ids* box click on *CSignalGenDlg*
In the *Messages* box click on   *WM_RButtonDown.*
Click on *Add Function* to add *OnRButtonDown*.
Click on *Edit Code* to see the function is a skeleton message handler.
Add Code 434 to the *OnRButtonDown* message handler.

Code 434 OnRButtonDown

```
void CSignalGenDlg::OnRButtonDown(UINT nFlags, CPoint point)
{
      CString strRightClick ;
      strRightClick = (CString)
      "Click on Clear to erase Number register and allow entry of a new
number."
      + "\n"
      + "Click on 0 to 9 to enter digits."
      + "\n"
      + "Click on . (dot) to enter a decimal point."
      + "\n"
      + "Click on <- to delete digits."
      + "\n"
      + "Click on CHS to change sign of number."
      + "\n"
      + "Click on Enter to enable storing a number in a parameter register."
      + "\n"
      + "Click any parameter button to store a parameter in the appropriate
register."
      + "\n"
      + "Such as Fixed, Begin, or End to store a frequency in Fixed, Start, or End
registers."
      + "\n"
      + "The max number of digits is 8. However max frequency is 50MHz"
      + "\n";
      MessageBox(strRightClick,"Click on buttons", MB_OK);
      CDialog::OnRButtonDown(nFlags, point);
}
```

4.10 Summary: Variables, Initialize Variables

Recapitulation of added variables to *SignalGenDlg.h*

```
class CSignalGenDlg : public CDialog
{
public:
      int m_cxChar;
      int m_cyChar;
      CFont m_fontMain;
      CFont m_fontMain1;

      BOOL m_bNew;
      BOOL m_bPosNumber;
      BOOL m_bEnable;
      BOOL m_bDecPt;

      int m_iLength;
      int m_iNumDigits;
      char m_char;
      double m_dNumber;

      double m_dFixed;
      double m_dBegin;
      double m_dEnd;
      double m_dTsec;

      double m_dNum;
      long m_lNum;
      long m_iNumber[40];

      double m_dVpp;
      double m_dOffset;
      double m_dDutyCycle;
      BOOL m_bSine;
      BOOL m_bPulse;
      BOOL m_bTriangle;

CString m_strNumber;      CString m_strFixed;      CString m_strBegin;
CString m_strEnd;         CString m_strTsec;       CString m_strDbmax;
CString m_strDbmin;       CString m_strDegmax;     CString m_strDegmin;
CString m_strVpp;         CString m_strOffset;     CString
m_strDutyCycle;
}
```

Initialized variables in *SignalGenDlg.cpp*

```
// CSignalGenDlg dialog
CSignalGenDlg::CSignalGenDlg(CWnd* pParent /*=NULL*/)
    : CDialog(CSignalGenDlg::IDD, pParent)
{
// init variables
    m_bNew = TRUE;              // enable storing digits into Number register
    m_bPosNumber = TRUE;
    m_bDecPt = FALSE;
    m_iNumDigits = 0;
    m_bEnable = FALSE;          // disable storing digits into any register

    m_dFixed = 555000;          // prevent program exit if no parameter.
    m_dBegin = 1;
    m_dEnd = 100000;
    m_dTsec = 10;

    m_dVpp = 2;                 // show waveform parameters
    m_dOffset = 0;
    m_dDutyCycle = 30;
    m_dDbmax = 0;
    m_dDbmin = -50;

    m_strNumber = _T("654321");
    m_strFixed = _T("555000");
    m_strBegin = _T("1");
    m_strEnd = _T("100000");
    m_strTsec = _T("10");

    m_strVpp = _T("2");
    m_strOffset = _T("0");
    m_strDutyCycle = _T("30");
}
```

5 Oscilloscope Front Panel Project

The intent is to design a two channel digital storage oscilloscope. The front panel contains the following controls (Figure 501).

1 Waveform screen display
    Voltage 8 vertical divisions
    Time 10 horizontal divisions.

2 Vertical controls – identical for 2 channels
    Select AC, DC, Ground – the channel input coupling.
    Select display screen Volts/Division – 2mv to 5v per division
    2, 5, 10, 20, 50, 100, 200, 500 mv per division
    1, 2, 5 volts per division.
    vertical position of zero volt sweep level

3. Sweep – Seconds/Division - time per division 5ns to 50s per division
    2, 5, 10, 20, 50, 100, 200, 500 ns per division
    1, 2, 5, 10, 20, 50, 100, 200, 500 ms per division
    1, 2, 5, 10, 20, 50 s per division
    Horizontal position of sweep

4. Trigger controls
    Select Trigger Source
        Channel 1, 2 AC or DC, AC line, external
    Select Trigger Type
        edge rise, edge fall, pulse normal, pulse inverted
    Select Level the amplitude level that the signal must cross to acquire a waveform.
    Select Norm, Auto trigger or View to see the trigger
    Position trigger level.

6. Menus - push buttons display specific menus to select from.
    Acquire, Cursor, Display, Filter, Math, Measure, Save/Load, Utility

7. Waveforms - push buttons display specific menus to select from
    Single, Run, Stop, Help

5.1 Create a dialog based project workspace.

Follow the procedure in Chapter 1, Section 1.3 except as follows.
Type the name *Oscilloscope* in the *Project Name* edit box.
Note addition of *Oscilloscope* in the *Location* edit box.
In step 2 of 4 type the title *Digital Storage Oscilloscope 50 MHz*

5.2 Build the *Oscilloscope* Project

Follow the procedure in Chapter 1, Section 1.4, page 4.

5.3 Change Dialog size and delete the OK and Cancel Buttons

Click on *File*, click on *Open* to get the *Open* dialog box
Change contents of the *Open as* edit box to *Text*
Click on *Oscilloscope.rc*
Click on Open to open the *.rc* file
Go to the file's *Dialog* section, and change
from
IDD_OSCILLOSCOPE_DIALOG DIALOGEX 0, 0, 320, 200
to
IDD_OSCILLOSCOPE_DIALOG DIALOGEX 0, 0, 675, 370

Click on File, click on *Save as* to get *Save as* dialog box, click on *Save*.
Close the *Oscilloscope.rc* file.

Click *ResourceView* at bottom of left pane.
Click on +Oscilloscope Resources.
Click on + Dialog.
Click on IDD_OSCILLOSCOPE_DIALOG.
Observe the new size of the dialog box (the front panel).

Click on the *OK* button. Right click, select cut to remove button
Click on the *Cancel* button. Right click, select cut to remove button
Click on the *text*. Right click, select cut to remove the text.

| *Emphasis: The dialog box is the front panel* |

Figure 501 Oscilloscope Front Panel Design

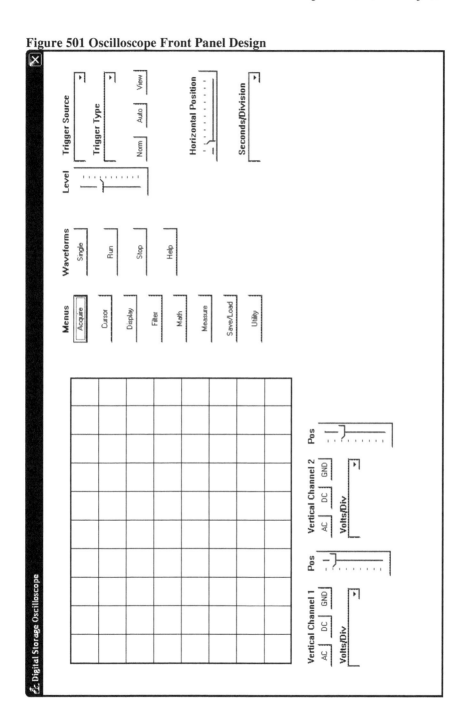

Figure 509 Oscilloscope Control Grid

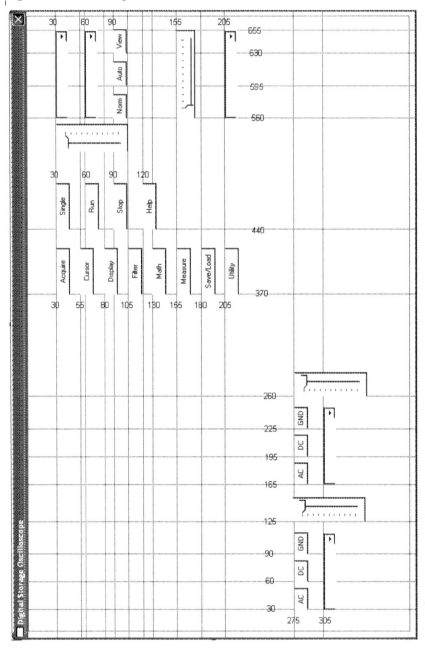

5.4 Code for Adding a Push Button

Show the *Front Panel* (Figure 501).
Click on left pane *ResourceView* tab. Click on +Oscilloscope Resources.
Click on +Dialog. Click on IDD_OSCILLOSCOPE_DIALOG to see the *"Digital Storage Oscilloscope 50 MHz"* front panel in the right hand pane.

Somewhere on the front panel is a box, the control tool box, containing symbols for the available controls [JP315]. To find out what control a symbol represents let the cursor hover over the symbol for a short time. A ToolTip will appear showing the name of the control associated with the symbol.

Add a control - push button example [JP319]
Drag a push button from the control tool box onto the front panel
Position the button[1] as the *Acquire* button (Figures 501, 509).
Right click on the button.
Click on *Properties*.

Figure 502

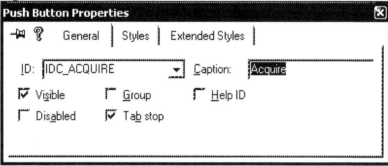

In the Push Button Properties dialog box (Figure 502) click on the *General* tab. There are 2 edit boxes *ID* and *Caption*, and 5 check boxes.
In the *Caption* edit box type *Acquire*. This is the push button title.
In the *ID* edit box erase *IDC_BUTTON*. Type *IDC_ACQUIRE* .
Only the check boxes *Visible* and *Tab stop* should be checked.
Click on the X to close the *Push Button Properties* box.

Note: if a button is the first button in a group check the group box.

---

[1] 4.4 Position a Control page 14

Add Push Button Functions for Message Passing

Click on View, click on Class Wizard, click on Message Maps [JP319].

Figure 503 Shows that many buttons have been added to the front panel

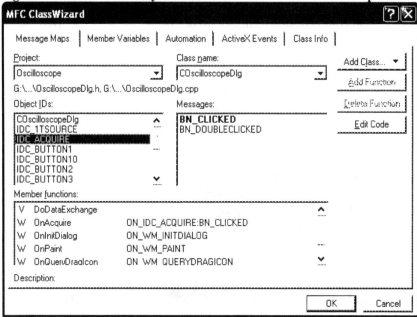

Verify Project is *Oscilloscope*; Class name is *COscilloscopeDlg* (Figure 503).

In the *Object IDs* box click on push button object id *IDC_ACQUIRE*.

In the *Messages* box click *BN_CLICKED*.

This activates the *Add Function* button.

Click on *Add Function* to get *Add Member function* box. Accept *Member function* name *OnAcquire*. Click on OK to install software. This adds code items 1, 2, 3.

1) to *OscilloscopeDlg.h* a prototype function *afx_msg void OnAcquire();*

2) to the message map in *OscilloscopeDlg.cpp* the function
ON_BN_CLICKED(IDC_ACQUIRE, OnAcquire)

3) in *OscilloscopeDlg.cpp* a skeleton message handler
void COscilloscopeDlg::OnAcquire( )

After menu and waveform buttons are programmed *OscilloscopeDlg.h* includes prototypes

```
afx_msg void OnAcquire();
afx_msg void OnCursor();
afx_msg void OnDisplay();
afx_msg void OnFilter();
afx_msg void OnMath();
afx_msg void OnMeasure();
afx_msg void OnSaveload();
afx_msg void OnUtility();
afx_msg void OnSingle();
afx_msg void OnStop();
afx_msg void OnRun();
afx_msg void OnHelp1();          // Add the 1 to avoid conflict with 6.0 help
```

and the message map in *OscilloscopeDlg.cpp* includes the functions

```
ON_BN_CLICKED(IDC_ACQUIRE, OnAcquire)
ON_BN_CLICKED(IDC_CURSOR, OnCursor)
ON_BN_CLICKED(IDC_DISPLAY, OnDisplay)
ON_BN_CLICKED(IDC_FILTER, OnFilter)
ON_BN_CLICKED(IDC_MATH, OnMath)
ON_BN_CLICKED(IDC_MEASURE, OnMeasure)
ON_BN_CLICKED(IDC_SAVELOAD, OnSaveload)
ON_BN_CLICKED(IDC_UTILITY, OnUtility)
ON_BN_CLICKED(IDC_SINGLE, OnSingle)
ON_BN_CLICKED(IDC_STOP, OnStop)
ON_BN_CLICKED(IDC_RUN, OnRun)
ON_BN_CLICKED(IDC_HELP1, OnHelp1)
```

and the skeleton message handlers

```
void COscilloscopeDlg::OnAcquire()
void COscilloscopeDlg::OnCursor()
void COscilloscopeDlg::OnDisplay()
void COscilloscopeDlg::OnFilter()
void COscilloscopeDlg::OnHelp1()
void COscilloscopeDlg::OnMath()
void COscilloscopeDlg::OnMeasure()
void COscilloscopeDlg::OnRun()
void COscilloscopeDlg::OnSaveload()
void COscilloscopeDlg::OnSingle()
void COscilloscopeDlg::OnStop()
void COscilloscopeDlg::OnUtility()
```

Programming with MFC

After channel input and trigger push buttons are programmed
OscilloscopeDlg.h includes prototypes
```
afx_msg void OnAc1();
afx_msg void OnAc2();
afx_msg void OnDc1();
afx_msg void OnDc2();
afx_msg void OnGnd1();
afx_msg void OnGnd2();

afx_msg void OnNorm();
afx_msg void OnAuto();
afx_msg void OnView();
```

and the message map in *OscilloscopeDlg.cpp* includes the functions
```
ON_BN_CLICKED(IDC_AC1, OnAc1)
ON_BN_CLICKED(IDC_AC2, OnAc2)
ON_BN_CLICKED(IDC_DC1, OnDc1)
ON_BN_CLICKED(IDC_DC2, OnDc2)
ON_BN_CLICKED(IDC_GND1, OnGnd1)
ON_BN_CLICKED(IDC_GND2, OnGnd2)

ON_BN_CLICKED(IDC_NORM, OnNorm)
ON_BN_CLICKED(IDC_AUTO, OnAuto)
ON_BN_CLICKED(IDC_VIEW, OnView)
```

and the skeleton message handlers
```
void COscilloscopeDlg::OnAc1()
void COscilloscopeDlg::OnAc2()
void COscilloscopeDlg::OnDc1()
void COscilloscopeDlg::OnDc2()
void COscilloscopeDlg::OnGnd1()
void COscilloscopeDlg::OnGnd2()

void COscilloscopeDlg::OnNorm()
void COscilloscopeDlg::OnAuto()
void COscilloscopeDlg::OnView()
```

Code for Button Message Handlers

Add push button code to *OscilloscopeDlg.cpp*.
Vertical channels AC1, DC1, GND1, AC2, DC2, GND2,
Controls SINGLE, RUN, STOP, HELP
Trigger NORM, AUTO, VIEW
The 6+4+3 = 13 push buttons have the same message handler code.

Add push button Code 501 to the AC1 message handler. Repeat for all push buttons except the menu buttons, which use property sheets (Chapter 6).

Code 501 Code for all push buttons

```
void COscilloscopeDlg::OnAc1()
{
  // send "AC1 button pressed" to hardware
  AfxMessageBox("AC1 pressed", MB_OK);          // message to output
}
```

The message box output temporarily replaces a message to hardware.

5.5 Code for Adding a Combo Box

Add a Control - Combo Box Example: (JP358)
  Drag a combo box from the control tool box to the front panel
  Position the combo box as the Trigger Source (Figures 501, 509).
  Right click on the Combo Box.
  Click on *Properties.*

Figure 504

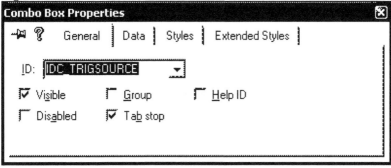

Click on the *General* tab (Figure 504).
  In the *ID* edit box erase IDC_COMBO1. Type IDC_TRIGSOURCE
    Only check the boxes *Visible* and *Tab Stop.*
Click on the *Data* tab. Type in four *listbox* items on four lines.
    Channel 1 AC, Channel 1 DC, Channel 2 AC, Channel 2 DC
    (use CTRL-ENTER to start a new line)
Click on the *Styles* tab.
    In *Type* box select *DropList,*
    In *Owner draw* box select *No,*
    Only check the box *Vertical scroll*

Extended Styles – no selections
   Click on the X to close the *Combo Box Properties* box.

On the front panel click on the combo box's *down arrow* at the right.
Pull down the bottom edge of the outline until the height is doubled. Do
this in order to show all listed items after a build. Build to see if pull
down was adequate. Modify accordingly.

Add Combo Box Functions for Message Passing Click on View, click
on Class Wizard, click on Message Maps [JP358].

Figure 505 Shows that combo boxes have been added to the front panel

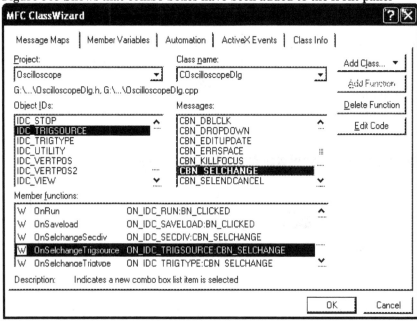

Verify Project is *Oscilloscope*, Class is *COscilloscopeDlg* (Figure 505).
In the *Object IDs* box click on object id *IDC_TRIGSOURCE*.
In the *Messages* box select *CBN_SELCHANGE*.
This activates the *Add Function* button.
Click on *Add Function* to get *Add Member function* box. Accept *Member
function* name *OnSelchangeTrigsource*. Click on OK to install software.
This adds code items 1, 2, 3.

1) to *OscilloscopeDlg.h* a prototype function
   afx_msg void OnSelchangeTrigsource( );

2) to the message and data maps in *OscilloscopeDlg.cpp* the function
   ON_CBN_SELCHANGE(IDC_TRIGSOURCE, OnSelchangeTrigsource)

3) in *OscilloscopeDlg.cpp* a skeleton message handler
   voidCOscilloscopeDlg::OnSelchangeTrigsource( )

Click on the *Data* tab for each combo box
Type in *listbox* items (use CTRL-ENTER to start a new line).

TRIGSOURCE
Channel 1 AC, Channel 1 DC, Channel 2 AC, Channel 2 DC

TRIGTYPE   *edge rise, edge fall, pulse normal, pulse inverted*

SECDIV   2, 5, 10, 20, 50, 100, 200, 500 ns per division
               1, 2, 5, 10, 20, 50, 100, 200, 500 micro s per division
               1, 2, 5, 10, 20, 50, 100, 200, 500 ms per division
               1, 2, 5, 10 s per division

VOLTSDIV1 and VOLTSDIV2
               2, 5, 10, 20, 50, 100, 200, 500 mv per division
               1, 2, 5, 10, 20, 50 volts per division.

Add 4 more combo boxes. After the combo boxes are programmed the
file *OscilloscopeDlg.h* includes the prototypes
  afx_msg void OnSelchangeVoltsdiv1();
  afx_msg void OnSelchangeVoltsdiv2();
  afx_msg void OnSelchangeSecdiv();
  afx_msg void OnSelchangeTrigsource();
  afx_msg void OnSelchangeTrigtype();

and the message map in *OscilloscopeDlg.cpp* includes the functions
  ON_CBN_SELCHANGE(IDC_VOLTSDIV1, OnSelchangeVoltsdiv1)
  ON_CBN_SELCHANGE(IDC_VOLTSDIV2, OnSelchangeVoltsdiv2)
  ON_CBN_SELCHANGE(IDC_SECDIV, OnSelchangeSecdiv)
  ON_CBN_SELCHANGE(IDC_TRIGSOURCE, OnSelchangeTrigsource)
  ON_CBN_SELCHANGE(IDC_TRIGTYPE, OnSelchangeTrigtype)

and the skeleton message handlers are
void COscilloscopeDlg::OnSelchangeVoltsdiv1()
void COscilloscopeDlg::OnSelchangeVoltsdiv2()
void COscilloscopeDlg::OnSelchangeSecdiv()
void COscilloscopeDlg::OnSelchangeTrigsource()
void COscilloscopeDlg::OnSelchangeTrigtype()

Code for Combo Box Message Handlers

Use ClassWizard to add variables so that DDX functions are added.

In the *Category* edit box select *Control* (Section 5.7 page 63).

Verify *Variable type* is *CComboBox*. Repeating for each combo box adds
a Code 502 line to *OscilloscopeDlg.h.*

Code 502 Combo Box Variables

```
CComboBox    m_wndCBsecdiv;
CComboBox    m_wndCBtrigsource;
CComboBox    m_wndCBtrigtype;
CComboBox    m_wndCBvoltsdiv2;
CComboBox    m_wndCBvoltsdiv1;
```

Add *public* string variables Code 503 to *OscilloscopeDlg.h* by hand.

Code 503 Combo Box String Variables

```
CString m_strSecDiv;
CString m_strVoltsdiv1;
CString m_strVoltsdiv2;
CString m_strTrigsource;
CString m_strTrigtype;
```

Add Combo Box message handler Code 504 to *OscilloscopeDlg.cpp.*

Code 504 Combo box message handler

```
void COscilloscopeDlg::OnSelchangeVoltsdiv1 ()       //  (JP329, 357)
{
    int nIndex = m_wndCBvoltsdiv1.GetCurSel ();
    if (nIndex != LB_ERR) {
      m_wndCBvoltsdiv1.GetLBText(nIndex, m_strVoltsdiv1);
    }
    AfxMessageBox (m_strVoltsdiv1, MB_OK);
}
```

Code 504 The items in a combo box list are numbered 1, 2, 3, ... MFC function *GetCurSel()* fetches the integer number of the selected item in the combo box list. *GetCurSel()* stores (returns) the number in *int* variable *nIndex*.

MFC function *GetLBText* uses nIndex to store in string variable *m_strVoltsdiv1* the selected volts/div item such as 50mv. The message box (50mv) output temporarily replaces a message that would be sent to the oscilloscope hardware.

m_wndCBvoltsdiv1 is a CComboBox variable, which means it can use *CComboBox::GetCurSel &CComboBox::GetLBText* member functions.

GetCurSel () retrieves the integer index of the currently selected item if any in the list box of a combo box. *CB_ERR* is returned if there are no items in the box, The integer index is stored in *nIndex*.

Knowing the index, *GetLBText* copies the item's text into CString variable *m_strVoltsdiv1*.

AfxMessageBox outputs the contents of CString *m_strVoltsdiv.*

5.6 Code for Adding a Slider

Add a Control. Sliders (aka TrackBars) Horizontal or Vertical are not really explained in JP932.
   Drag a slider from the control tool box to the front panel
   Position the slider at Vertical Channel 1 Pos (Figures 501, 509).
   Right click on the slider.
   Click on *Properties*.

Figure 506 Selecting a Vertical Slider

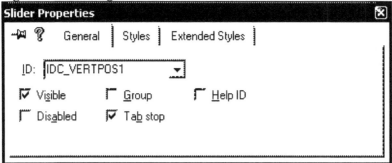

Note: The control tool box only has a horizontal slider. However a vertical or horizontal slider is selected in the Styles tab (Figure 506).

   Click on the *General* tab.
   In the *ID* edit box erase IDC_COMBO1. Type IDC_VERTPOS1
   Only check the boxes *Visible* and *Tab Stop*.

   Click on the *Styles* tab.
   In *Orientation* box select- *Vertical*.
   In *Point* box select *Top/Left*.
      (the thumb pointer is at the top and points left)
   Only check the boxes *Tick marks, Auto ticks*

   Click on the *Extended Styles* tab
   Only check *Modal frame*.
   Click on the X to close the *Slider Properties* box.

In the Oscilloscope dialog box (the front panel) the slider does not appear to be vertical, because you have to reduce width and increase height by dragging edges. Add 3 sliders per Figs 501, 509. Add *IDC_VERTPOS2, IDC_HORZPOS, IDC_TRIGLEVEL*.

Add Slider Functions for Message Passing

Click on View, click on Class Wizard, click on Message Maps [JP932].

Figure 507 Shows that WM_HSCROLL message has been added

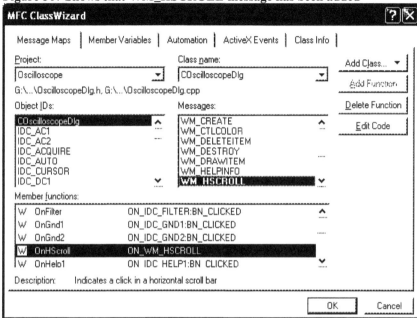

Verify Project is *Oscilloscope*, Class is *COscilloscopeDlg* (Figure 507).
In the *Object IDs* box click on *COscilloscopeDlg*
In the *Messages* box click *WM_HSCROLL*
This activates the *Add Function* button.
Click on *Add Function* to get *Add Member function* box. Accept *Member function* name *OnHScroll*. Click on OK to install software. This adds code items 1, 2, 3. Repeat for *VScroll*

1) to *OscilloscopeDlg.h* a prototype function
afx_msg void OnHScroll(UINT nSBCode, UINT nPos, CScrollBar pScrollBar);*

2) to the message map in *OscilloscopeDlg.cpp* the function
    ON_WM_HSCROLL()

3) in *OscilloscopeDlg.cpp* a skeleton message handler
void COscilloscopeDlg::OnHScroll(UINT nSBCode, UINT nPos, CScrollBar pScrollBar)*

Use ClassWizard to add variables (Section 5.7 page 63) so that DDX functions are added. Verify *Variable type* is *CComboBox*. Repeating for each slider adds slider variables Code 505 to *OscilloscopeDlg,h*.

Code 505 Slider Variables added via ClassWizard

```
CSliderCtrl m_wndStriglevel;
CSliderCtrl m_wndShorzpos;
CSliderCtrl m_wndSvpos2;
CSliderCtrl m_wndSvpos1;
```

After HICON add *public* string variables and prototype Code 506 to *OscilloscopeDlg.h* by hand.

Code 506 Slider Prototype and String Variables

```
void InitSliders ();
CString m_strTriglevel;
CString m_strHorzpos;
CString m_strVpos2;
CString m_strVpos1;
```

Initialize each slider's range, thumb position, and tic marks.
Add Code 507 to *OscilloscopeDlg* after *OnQueryDragIcon()*.

Code 507 Initialize Sliders

```
void COscilloscopeDlg::InitSliders ( )    // (JP935, 955)
{
    m_wndSvpos1.SetRange (0, 80); // draws tick marks at start and end of range
    m_wndSvpos1.SetPos (10);        // positions thumb at mark 10
    m_wndSvpos1.SetTicFreq (10);   // shows tick marks at 0, 10, 20, ... 70, 80
        m_wndSvpos2.SetRange (0, 80);
        m_wndSvpos2.SetPos (20);
        m_wndSvpos2.SetTicFreq (10);
    m_wndShorzpos.SetRange (0, 50); // Sets slider min and max position
    m_wndShorzpos.SetPos (5);        // Sets current position of the slider thumb
    m_wndShorzpos.SetTicFreq (5);   // Sets tick marks units separation
        m_wndStriglevel.SetRange (0, 50);
        m_wndStriglevel.SetPos (15);
        m_wndStriglevel.SetTicFreq (5);
}
```

A range of 50 will have 1+10 tic marks when set tic freq = 5.

Sliders message handlers *HSCROLL* and *VSCROLL* are the de facto message handlers for sliders.

When a slider thumb is moved, or clicked on, the slider sends the messages *WM_VSCROLL* or *WM_HSCROLL*.

Add Code 508 to OnHScroll in *OscilloscopeDlg.cpp*.

Code 508 OnHScroll

```
void COscilloscopeDlg::OnHScroll(UINT nSBCode, UINT nPos, CScrollBar*
pScrollBar)
{
  pScrollBar->GetDlgCtrlID();
  if(nSBCode == SB_THUMBPOSITION) {
    m_strHorzpos.Format("%ld", nPos);
    AfxMessageBox (m_strHorzpos, MB_OK);    // send pos to the hardware.

    UpdateData(false);
  }
  else {CDialog::OnHScroll(nSBCode, nPos, pScrollBar);
  }

  CDialog::OnHScroll(nSBCode, nPos, pScrollBar);
}
```

SB_THUMBPOSITION is a *VScroll* and *HScroll* parameter (use F1). The current position is specified by the *nPos* parameter.

Each click on or movement of a thumb on a slider sends a message to *OnHScroll* or *OnVScroll*. Clicking anywhere on a slider scale moves the thumb to that position. Clicking on the thumb, *holding the mouse button down* while moving the thumb to another position, and then releasing the mouse button produces a message.

Each movement of a thumb on any slider creates a message to *OnHScroll* or *OnVScroll*. Consequently a switch statement is required so that each slider is assigned a case.

GetDlgCtrlID is an MFC function.

Add Code 509 to OnVScroll in *OscilloscopeDlg.cpp*.
Code 509 OnVScroll

```
void COscilloscopeDlg::OnVScroll(UINT nSBCode, UINT nPos, CScrollBar*
pScrollBar)
{
  // TODO: Add your message handler code here and/or call default
    switch(pScrollBar->GetDlgCtrlID()) {
    case IDC_TRIGLEVEL:
      if(nSBCode == SB_THUMBPOSITION) {
        m_strTriglevel.Format("%ld", nPos);
        AfxMessageBox(m_strTriglevel, MB_OK);

        UpdateData(false);
      }
      else {CDialog::OnHScroll(nSBCode, nPos, pScrollBar);
      }
      break;

    case IDC_VERTPOS1:
      if(nSBCode == SB_THUMBPOSITION) {
        m_strVpos1.Format("%ld", nPos);
        AfxMessageBox(m_strVpos1, MB_OK);

        UpdateData(false);
      }
      else {CDialog::OnHScroll(nSBCode, nPos, pScrollBar);
      }
      break;

    case IDC_VERTPOS2:
      if(nSBCode == SB_THUMBPOSITION) {
        m_strVpos2.Format("%ld", nPos);
        AfxMessageBox(m_strVpos2, MB_OK);

        UpdateData(false);
      }
      else {CDialog::OnHScroll(nSBCode, nPos, pScrollBar);
      }
      break;
    }

  CDialog::OnVScroll(nSBCode, nPos, pScrollBar);
}
```

5.7 Code for Combo Box and Slider Variables

Member variables to be used in the message handlers are added via *Class Wizard* in the Member Variable tab.

> Addition of one variable is illustrated here. Add additional variables when message handlers are implemented.

Figure 508

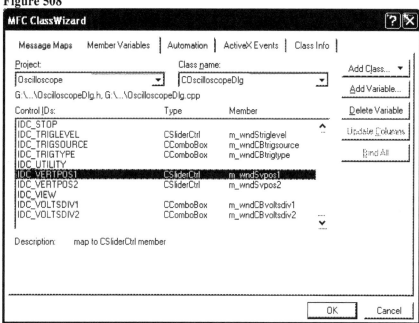

Click on View, click Class Wizard, click Member Variables tab.
Check project is *Oscilloscope*, class name is *COscilloscopeDlg*
In the *Control IDs* box click on *IDC_VERTPOS1*.
 Click on *Add Variable* to get *Add Member Variable* dialog box.
 Enter member variable name *m_wndSvpos1*
 Click on *Category*. Select *control*. Click on OK. To install code.

This adds code items 1, 2.
1) to *OscilloscopeDlg.h* a variable *CSliderCtrl m_wndSvpos1;*

2) to *OscilloscopeDlg.cpp*
   DDX_Control(pDX, IDC_VERTPOS1, m_wndSvpos1);

5.8 Code for Support functions

Add prototype Code 509 to *OscilloscopeDlg.h*.
Code 508

```
void CrtScreen ();
```

Add display screen define Code 510 to *OscilloscopeDlg.cpp*.
Code 510 Display Screen Defines

```
//crt screen
#define u0   50
#define v0   45
#define u1   500
#define v1   405
#define u2   400
#define HOUT 10
#define VOUT 8
```

Add display screen Code 511 to *OnPaint* in *OscilloscopeDlg.cpp*.
Code 511 OnPaint

```
void COscilloscopeDlg::OnPaint()
{
  CPaintDC dc(this); // device context for painting
  dc.SetBkMode(TRANSPARENT);
  dc.TextOut (u0+145, v1+23, "Pos");
  dc.TextOut (u0+345, v1+23, "Pos");
  dc.TextOut (u0, v1+23, "Vertical Channel 1");
  dc.TextOut (u0+205, v1+23, "Vertical Channel 2");
  dc.TextOut (u0+0,  v1+75, "Volts/Div");
  dc.TextOut (u0+205, v1+75, "Volts/Div");
  dc.TextOut (u2+450, v1-90, "Seconds/Division");
  dc.TextOut (u2+450, v1-170, "Horizontal Position");
  dc.TextOut (u2+450, v0-17, "Trigger Source");
  dc.TextOut (u2+450, v0+50-17, "Trigger Type");
  dc.TextOut (u2+390, v0-17, "Level");
  dc.TextOut (u1+70, v0-17, "Menus");
  dc.TextOut (u1+170, v0-17, "Controls");
  CrtScreen ();
  CDialog::OnPaint();
} //end of OnPaint
```

Add crt screen Code 512 to *OscilloscopeDlg.cpp.*
Code 512 CrtScreen

```
void COscilloscopeDlg::CrtScreen ()      // nlp
{
  CClientDC dc(this); // device context for painting

  // select body brush color
  CBrush brush (RGB (255, 255, 230));
  CBrush* pOldBrush = dc.SelectObject (&brush);

  // create black solid pen
  CPen pen1 (PS_SOLID, 2, RGB (0, 0, 0,));  // (JP 60, 61)
  CPen* pOldPen1 = dc.SelectObject (&pen1);

  // K-Draw the body of the Output display.
  dc.Rectangle (u0, v0, u1, v1);

  // create gray solid pen   //light gray (JP 60, 61)
  CPen pen0 (PS_SOLID, 1, RGB (130, 130, 130,));
  CPen* pOldPen0 = dc.SelectObject (&pen0);

  // Draw H and V lines
  int dx=(u1 - u0)/HOUT;
  int dy=(v1 - v0)/VOUT;
  int i;

  // H-Draw the Output horizontal lines.
  for (i=1; i<VOUT; i++)
  {
    dc.MoveTo(u0, v0+(dy*i));
    dc.LineTo(u1, v0+(dy*i));
  }

  // H-Draw the Output vertical lines.
  for (i=1; i<HOUT; i++)
  {
    dc.MoveTo(u0+(dx*i), v0);
    dc.LineTo(u0+(dx*i), v1);
  }

  return;
} //end of CrtScreen
```

5.9 A Simple Help Program

This is the simple help system. A right mouse click accesses it (JP102).

This is for a mouse action
Click on *View*, click on *Class Wizard*, click on *Message Maps*.
Verify Project is *Oscilloscope*, Class name is *COscilloscopeDlg*.
In the *Object Ids* box click on *COscilloscopeDlg*
In the *Messages* box click on *WM_RButtonDown*.
Click on *Add Function* to add *OnRButtonDown*
Click on *Edit Code* to see function added as a skeleton message handler.
Add following code to the message handler.
Code 514 OnRButtonDown

```
void CSignalGenDlg::OnRButtonDown(UINT nFlags, CPoint point)
{
    CString strRightClick ;
  strRightClick = (CString)              // casts text into a string
    "Set up a vertical channel input by selecting AC, DC , or GND."
    + "\n"
    + " Use Pos to set up a vertical channel zero signal line on the screen."
    + "\n"
    + "Select Volts/Div vertical scale for each channel."
    + "\n"
    + "Select the Trigger Source."
    + "\n"
    + "Select the Trigger Type."
    + "\n"
    + "Set the trigger Level and select Norm, Auto, or View trigger format."
    + "\n"
    + "Select Seconds/Division for the horizontal sweep speed."
    + "\n"
    + "Use Horizontal Position to adjust sweep position after a signal appears."
    + "\n"
    + "The Menus show features available for oscilloscope operation."
    + "\n"
    + "Select Controls – single sweep, run continuously, stop, or get help."
    ;
    MessageBox(strRightClick,"Help", MB_OK);      // (JP116)

    CDialog::OnRButtonDown(nFlags, point);
}
```

6 Design a Property Sheet connected to a Menu Button

This design project shows how to create a property sheet with four property pages (JP449) that is accessed via a button in the File menu.

The property sheet has four property pages in the form of dialog boxes. Property page 1 has a push button added as an example.

Important: The property sheet **is not a dialog box** (Section 6.5 page 71).

6.1 Create the *PropSheetMenu* Workspace

Follow the procedure in Chapter 1, Section 1.1 page 1 for *Single Document* except as follows.
Type the name *PropSheetMenu* in the *Project Name* edit box.
Note addition of *PropSheetMenu* in the *Location* edit box.

6.2 Build the *PropSheetMenu* Project

Follow the procedure in Chapter 1, Section 1.4 page 4.

Notes:
After adding code to any file repeat 6.2 to check for errors.

Figure 601 The "empty" Window

Figure 602 Property Sheet

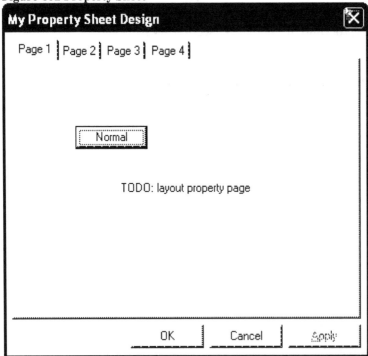

6.3 Use *ResourceView* to create four Property Page Dialog Boxes

1 Click ResourceView Tab in left pane.
   Click + to left of *PropSheetMenu Resources*.
   Click + to left of *Dialog*. See IDD_ABOUTBOX

2 Click *Insert* in menu bar at top of screen, Click *Resource*
   Click on *Dialog* in the *Insert Resource* dialog box.
   Click on + next to *Dialog*.
   Click on *IDD_Proppage_Large*
   Click on *New*.
IDD_PROPPAGE_LARGE appears in the left pane, and the *Property Page* dialog box appears in right pane.

3 Right click in the *Property Page* dialog box. Click on *Properties* to get the *Dialog Properties* box (Figure 603).

Figure 603 Page 1 Properties

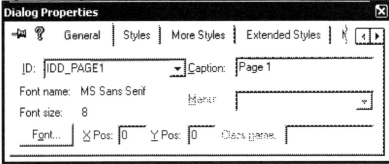

Change ID box IDD_PROPPAGE_LARGE to IDD_PAGE1
Change caption box to *Page 1*
Do not change anything else.
Click on X. IDD_PAGE1 appears in the left pane.
Dialog box title is now *Page 1*

4 Repeat 2 and 3 with IDD_PAGE2 and *Page 2*.

5 Repeat 2 and 3 with IDD_PAGE3 and *Page 3*.

6 Repeat 2 and 3 with IDD_PAGE4 and *Page 4*.

6.4 Use *ClassWizard* to create four pairs of Property Page files

1 In the *ResourceView* Pane, click on +PropSheetMenu resources, click on +Dialog.

2 Click on IDD_PAGE1

3 In the *View* menu click *ClassWizard* to open *MFC ClassWizard*.
Select the *Message Maps* tab. The *Adding a Class* dialog *box* appears.

4 Click OK in the *Adding a Class* dialog *box*.
   Type *CPage1* in the Name edit box
   Select *CPropertyPage* in the Base Class edit box.
   Verify that the Dialog ID box contains IDD_PAGE1.
   Click on *OK*.
   Click on *OK*.
   Click on *FileView* to see new files *Page1.h* and *Page1.cpp*.

3 Click on IDD_PAGE2. Repeat 3, and 4 for *CPage2*.

4 Click on IDD_PAGE3. Repeat 3, and 4 for *CPage3*.

5 Click on IDD_PAGE4. Repeat 3, and 4 for *CPage4*.

6.5 Use *ClassWizard* to create a Property Sheet

1 In the *View* menu click on *ClassWizard* to open *MFC ClassWizard*.
Select the *Message Maps* tab. See [JP449].

2 Click on *Add Class, then click on New* to open *New Class* dialog box.
Type *CMyPropertySheet* in the Name edit box.
Select *CPropertySheet* in the Base Class edit box.
Click on *OK*. Click on *OK* to close *ClassWizard*.
In Fileview see new files *MyPropertySheet.h* and *.cpp*.

3 Add code to *MyPropertySheet.h*.
Add Code 601 after the line // *MyPropertySheet.h : header file*.
Code 601 Includes

```
#include "Page1.h"
#include "Page2.h"
#include "Page3.h"
#include "Page4.h"
```

Add Code 602 after the line *DECLARE_DYNAMIC(CMyPropertySheet)*.
Code 602

```
public:
CPage1 m_Page1;
CPage2 m_Page2;
CPage3 m_Page3;
CPage4 m_Page4;
```

4 In Fileview click on *MyPropertySheet.cpp*.
Add Code 603 to the first two functions following // *CMyPropertySheet*
Code 603

```
AddPage(&m_Page1);
AddPage(&m_Page2);
AddPage(&m_Page3);
AddPage(&m_Page4);
```

5 Verify that the following code is at the top of *MyPropertySheet.cpp*
#include " MyPropertySheet.h"

6.6 Menu Items

1) Click *ResourceView* pane. Click on *+Menu*, click on
IDR_MAINFRAME.

2) In the menu bar, right click on *New* in the *File* menu.
  Right click on *Properties.*
  change the ID to *ID_FILE_PROPSHEET*
  change the caption to *&PropSheet\tCtrl+P*
  Click on X

3) Create a message handler for the *PropSheet* menu item.

In the C++ *View* menu click on *ClassWizard.*
  Verify that Project is *PropSheetMenu*, and class name is *CMainFrame.*
  In Object ID click on *ID_FILE_PROPSHEET*
  In Messages click on *COMMAND.*
  Click on *Add Function* to get *Add Member function* box.
  OnFilePropSheet appears in the *Add Member Functions* box.
  Click on OK.
  Click on Edit code button to get *OnFilePropsheet* in *MainFrm.cpp.*

Add *#include "MyPropertySheet.h"* at the top of *MainFrm.cpp.*

Verify *ON_COMMAND(ID_FILE_PROPSHEET, OnFilePropsheet)* is
in the *MainFrm.cpp* message map.

Add Code 604 to *OnFilePropsheet()* in *MainFrm.cpp.*
Code 604 OnFilePropsheet

```
void CMainFrame:OnFilePropsheet()
{
    CMyPropertySheet  propsh(_T("My Property Sheet Design"));
    propsh.DoModal(); \
}
// Note: propsh is a convenient fake word used here.
```

Verify that *afx_msg void OnFilePropsheet();* is in the *MainFrm.cpp.*
message map.

6.7 Add Controls to the Property Pages

Select the *ResourceView* tab in Visual C++.
Click on + Dialog. Click on IDD_PAGE1.

Example: Add a push button to property page 1.
Right click on the button to get a menu. Click on *Properties*.
Change Caption to *Normal* and the ID to *IDC_NORMAL*. Click on the X.

Right click on the Normal button to get a menu.
Click on *ClassWizard*.
Verify Project is *PropSheetMenu*, and Class Name is *CPage1*.
In Object IDs click on *IDC_NORMAL*
In Messages click on *BN_CLICKED*.
Click on *Add Function* button.
OnNormal appears in Member Functions box. Click on OK.
Click on Edit code button to get the (skeleton code) message handler
void Page1::OnNormal( ). No code is added at this time.

Click on Page1.cpp to find in the message map.
ON_BN_CLICKED(IDC_NORMAL, OnNormal)

Click on *Page1.h* to find the prototype *afx_msg void OnNormal();*.

Build and execute *PropSheetMenu.exe*.
Click on File menu. Click on PropSheet item.
"My Property Sheet Design" dialog box appears.

6.8 Convert to Wizard
This is an option

```
// add one line and build
void CMainFrame:OnFilePropsheet()
{
    CMyPropertySheet  propsh(_T("My Property Sheet Design"));
    propsh.SetWizardMode();
    propsh.DoModal(); \
}
```

7 Design a Property Sheet connected to a Dialog Box

This design project shows how to create a property sheet with two property pages accessed by a push button in a dialog box [JP449]. The dialog box has an Acquire button, which accesses the property sheet (Figure 701).

7.1 Create the *PropSheetDialog* Workspace

Follow the procedure in Chapter 1 Section 1.3 page 3 for *Dialog Based* except as follows.
　　Type the name *PropSheetDialog* in the *Project Name* edit box.
　　Note addition of *PropSheetDialog* in the *Location* edit box.

7.2 Build the *PropSheetDialog* Project

Follow the procedure in Chapter 1, Section 1.4.

Figure 702 shows the Acquire property pages.

Note: After adding code to any file repeat 7.2 to check for errors.

Figure 701 Property Sheet dialog

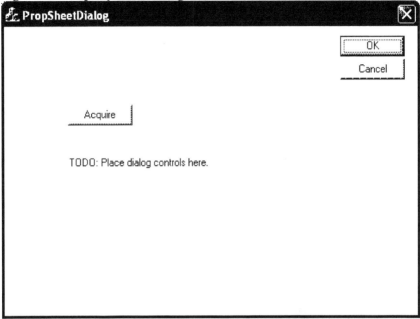

Figure 702 The Acquire Property Pages

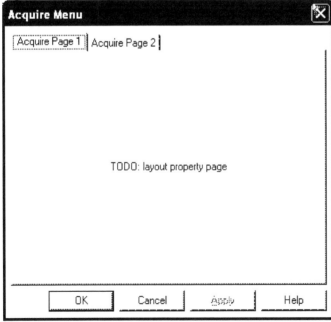

7.3 Use *ResourceView* to create two Property Page Dialog Boxes

1 Click *ResourceView* Tab in left pane.
  Click +DialogButton *Resources*.
  Click +Dialog.
  Double click on IDD_PROPSHEETDIALOG_DIALOG

2 Click *Insert* in menu bar at top of screen, Click *Resource*
  Click on +*Dialog* in *Insert Resource* dialog box.
  Click on *IDD_Proppage_Large*
  Click on *New*.
IDD_PROPPAGE_LARGE appears in the left pane.
The *Property Page* dialog box appears in right pane.

3 Right click in the *Property Page* dialog box. Click on *Properties* to get
the *Dialog Properties* box

Figure 703 Acquire Page 1 Properties

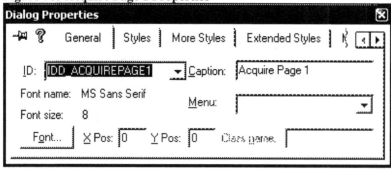

  Change ID box IDD_DIALOG to IDD_ACQUIREPAGE1
  Change caption box to *Acquire Page 1*
  Click on X.

4 Repeat 2 and 3 with IDD_ACQUIREPAGE2 and *Acquire Page 2*.

7.4 Use *ClassWizard* to create two pairs of Property Page files

1 In the *ResourceView* Pane click on +Dialog

2 This is important. Click on IDD_ACQUIREPAGE1

3 In the *View* menu click *ClassWizard*.

4 Click OK in the *Adding a Class* dialog *box*.
  Type *CAcquirePage1* in the Name edit box
  Select *CPropertyPage* in the Base Class edit box.
  Verify Dialog ID box contains IDD_ACQUIREPAGE1.
  Click on *OK*.
  Click on *OK*.
  In FileView to see new files AcquirePage1.h and AcquirePage1.cpp.

3 Click on IDD_ACQUIREPAGE2. Repeat 3, and 4 for *CAcquirePage2*.

7.5 Use *ClassWizard* to create a Property Sheet

1 In the *View* menu click on *ClassWizard*.
  Select the *Message Maps* tab. Verify project is *PropSheetDialog*.

2 Click on *Add Class, and then click on New* to open *New Class* dialog
box (JP449). Ignore the Dialog ID box (JP449, 451).
    Type *CAcquirePropertySheet* in the Name edit box.
    Select *CPropertySheet* in the Base Class edit box.
    Click on *OK*. Click on *OK* to close *Classwizard*.
    In Fileview see new files *AcquirePropertySheet.h* and *.cpp*.

3 Add code to *AcquirePropertySheet.h*.

Add Code 701 below the line // *AcquirePropertySheet.h. : header file*
Code 701

```
#include "AcquirePage1.h"
#include "AcquirePage2.h"
```

Add code 702 after *DECLARE_DYNAMIC(CAcquirePropertySheet)*.
Code 702

```
public:
CAcquirePage1 m_AcquirePage1;
CAcquirePage2 m_AcquirePage2;
```

4 Add code to *AcquirePropertySheet.cpp*.

Add Code 703 to the first two functions after // CAcquirePropertySheet
Code 703

```
AddPage(&m_AcquirePage1);
AddPage(&m_AcquirePage2);
```

5 Verify that the following code is in *AcquirePropertySheet.cpp*
    #include " AcquirePropertySheet.h"

6 In *PropertySheetDlg.cpp* add *#include "AcquirePropertySheet.h"* at the
top of the file.

7.6 Add the Acquire Push Button to the dialog box

Show the *Front Panel* (Figure 701).
Click on left pane *ResourceView* tab. Click on +Dialog.
Double click on IDD_PROPSHEETDIALOG

Add a control - push button example [JP319]
Drag a push button from the control tool box onto the front panel
Position the button[1] according to the front panel design (Figure 701).
Right click on the button. Click on *Properties*.
Change caption to *Acquire* and the ID to *IDC_ACQUIRE*. Click on the X

Right click on the button to get a menu.
Click on *ClassWizard*. Verify Project is *PropSheetDialog*, and Class Name is *PropSheetDialogDlg*.
In Object IDs click on *IDC_ACQUIRE*
In Messages click on *BN_CLICKED*.
Click on *Add Function* button.
OnAcquire appears in Member Functions box.
Click on Edit code button to get *PropSheetDialogDlg.cpp* and find skeleton code for the message handler function
CPropSheetDialogDlg::OnAcquire( )

And added to the *PropSheetDialogDlg.cpp* message map is
ON_BN_CLICKED(IDC_ACQUIRE, OnAcquire)

Click on *PropSheetDialogDlg..h* to find the prototype
afx_msg void OnAcquire();

Add Code 704 to *CPropSheetDialogDlg::OnAcquire( )* as follows
Code 704 OnAcquire

```
void CPropSheetDialogDlg::OnAcquire( )
{
  CAcquirePropertySheet ps(_T("Acquire Menu"),NULL, 0);
// ps.SetWizardMode();     // add this line to convert to wizard if you wish
  ps.DoModal();
}
```

---

[1] 4.4 Position a Control page 14

8 More About Sliders

This design project shows how to connect a slider to an edit box that displays the slider's position (JP933), and shows how to write code when there is more than one slider in the same dialog box.

8.1 Create a Dialog Based Project Workspace

Follow the procedure in Chapter 1, Section 1.3 Dialog Based except as follows.

Type the name *Slider* in the *Project Name* edit box.
Note addition of *Slider* in the *Location* edit box.
In step 2 of 4 screen type the title *Slider Example*.

8.2 Build the *Slider* Project

Follow the procedure in Chapter 1, Section 1.4
Note: After adding code to any file repeat 8.2 to check for errors.

Figure 801 Slider Project

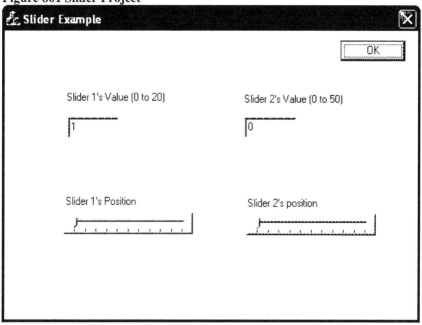

Figure 802 Slider Dialog Control Positions

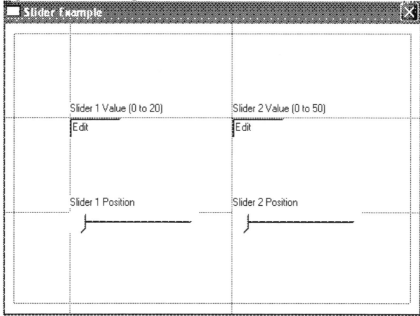

8.3 Add Controls to Slider Example Dialog Box

1) Click on the *Cancel* button. Right click, select cut to remove button
Click on the *text box*. Right click, select cut to remove the text.

2) Drag four static texts from the control tool box to the dialog box.
Position them per Figure 802. Right click on each static text box, and in
the Caption box type the text per Figure 802.

3) Drag two edit boxes from the control tool box to the dialog box.
Position them per Figure 802. Right click on each edit box, and in the ID
boxes type IDC_SLIDER_VALUE1 and IDC_SLIDER_VALUE2.

4) Drag two slider controls from the control tool box to the dialog box.
Position them per Figure 802. Right click on an edit box, and in the ID
box type IDC_SLIDER1. In the Styles Tab select *Bottom/right* for *Point*.
Check *Tick Marks* and *Auto Ticks*. Repeat with IDC_SLIDER2, etc.

5) Right-click in the current dialog and select ClassWizard (Figure 803).
Member variables to be used in the message handlers are added via *Class
Wizard* in the Member Variables tab.

Figure 803 Adding Member Variables

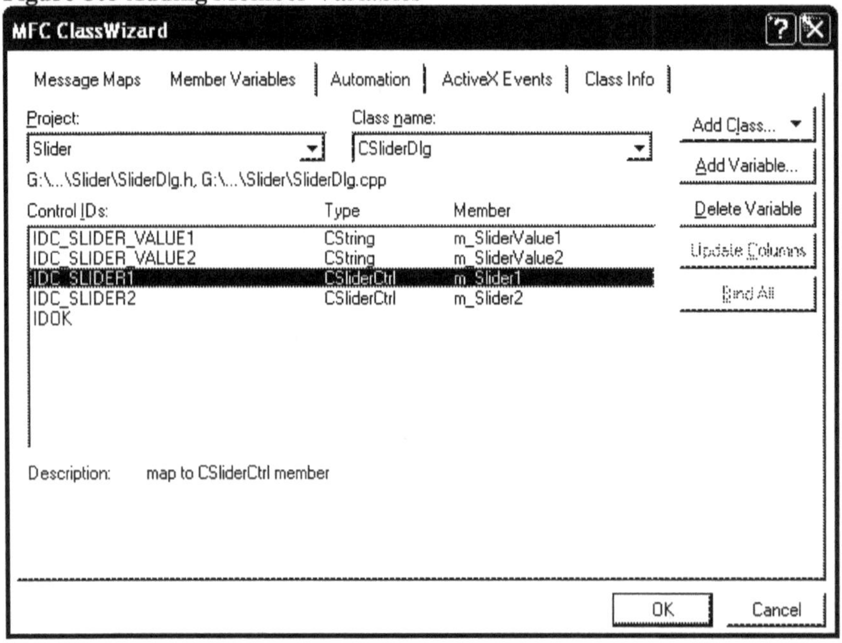

6) Click Member Variables tab.

Check project is *Slider*, class name is *CSliderDlg*

In the *Control IDs* box click on *IDC_SLIDER1*.

  Click on *Add Variable* to get *Add Member Variable* dialog box.

  Enter member variable name *m_Slider1*

  Click on *Category*. Select *Control*. Note: *Variable type is CSliderCtrl*.

  Click on OK. Click on OK.

  Repeat for variable *m_Slider2*

This adds code items a, b.

a) to *sliderDlg.h* under Dialog Data   *CSliderCtrl m_Slider1;* and 2

b) to *sliderDlg.cpp*

      DDX_Control(pDX, IDC_SLIDER1, m_Slider1); and 2

7) Add variables *m_SliderValue1, m_SliderValue2*.

Click on *Category,* Select *Value*. For variable type select *CString*.

8) Open the MFC ClassWizard dialog box, and click Message Maps.

In the Object IDs list box, click *CSliderDlg*. In the list of Member Functions, click WM_INITDIALOG. Click the *Edit Code* button.

Add Code 801 to *OnInitDialog* after the *TODO* line.

Code 801 The slider control parameters

```
m_Slider1.SetRange(0,20);
m_Slider1.SetTicFreq (2);
m_SliderValue1 = "1";
UpdateData(FALSE);

m_Slider2.SetRange(0,50);
m_Slider2.SetTicFreq (5);
m_SliderValue2 = "0";
UpdateData(FALSE);
```

9) As explained in 5.6 page 58, sliders communicate via HScroll and VScroll. Code 802 simply reads slider positions into the slider value variables.

In the Object IDs list box, click *CSliderDlg*. In the list of Messages, click *WM_HSCROLL*. Click *Edit Code*. Add the *OnHScroll* code 802.

Add Code 802 to OnHScroll in SliderDlg.cpp.

Code 802 OnHScroll

```
void CSliderDlg::OnHScroll(UINT nSBCode, UINT nPos, CScrollBar*
pScrollBar)
{
  // TODO: Add your message handler code here and/or call default
    switch(pScrollBar ->GetDlgCtrlID()) {
    case IDC_SLIDER1:
        if(nSBCode == SB_THUMBPOSITION) {
          m_SliderValue1.Format("%ld", nPos);
          UpdateData(false);
        }
        else {CDialog::OnHScroll(nSBCode, nPos, pScrollBar);
        }
        break;

    case IDC_SLIDER2:
        if(nSBCode == SB_THUMBPOSITION) {
          m_SliderValue2.Format("%ld", nPos);
          UpdateData(false);
        }
        else {CDialog::OnHScroll(nSBCode, nPos, pScrollBar);
        }
        break;
    }
}
```

10) The code that connects slider position to the edit boxes are the DDX functions (JP397). DDX functions map control data to member variables. Class Wizard automatically installs DDX functions (steps 6 and 7). Here is code taken from SliderDlg.cpp

```
void CSliderDlg::DoDataExchange(CDataExchange* pDX)
{
  CDialog::DoDataExchange(pDX);
  //{{AFX_DATA_MAP(CSliderDlg)
  DDX_Control(pDX, IDC_SLIDER2, m_Slider2);
  DDX_Control(pDX, IDC_SLIDER1, m_Slider1);
  DDX_Text(pDX, IDC_SLIDER_VALUE1, m_SliderValue1);
  DDX_Text(pDX, IDC_SLIDER_VALUE2, m_SliderValue2);
  //}}AFX_DATA_MAP
}
```

9 Tic Tac Toe - a Document/View Project

The goal here is to understand the *document/view* architecture. We recast JP's Tic Tac program [JP106] as a *single document/view* project named *TicTacToe* by using AppWizard and ClassWizard.

The Tic Tac Toe game board consists of a 3 x 3 array of squares (Figure 901). One player writes X's in the squares. A second player writes O's in the squares. The program guarantees players take turns. After each X or O is placed the game checks for a winner or a draw. A winner has placed three X's, or O's, in a horizontal row, a vertical row, or a diagonal. A draw occurs when 9 squares are filled and there is no winner.

Clicking the left mouse button over an empty square places an X in the square. Clicking the right mouse button over an empty square places an O in the square.

Double clicking the left mouse button over any grid line clears the board, and starts a new game, or click on *Reset* in the *File* menu.

Figure 901 Tic Tac Toe Window

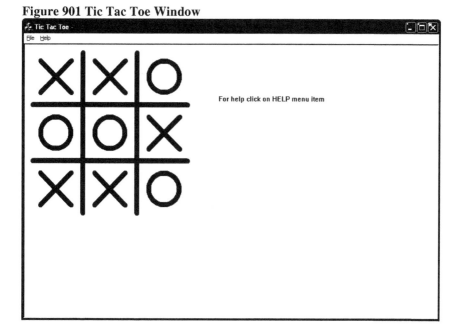

9.1 Create the *TicTacToe* project Workspace

Follow the procedure in Chapter 1, Section 1.1 for a single document project.
> Type the name *TicTacToe* in the *Project Name* edit box.
> Note addition of *TicTacToe* in the *Location* edit box.

This is different - in Step 4 click the *Advance* button. Type *tic* in the File Extension box. This defines the file name extension for files in this project.

9.2 Build and Execute the *TicTacToe* Project

Follow the procedure in Chapter 1, Section 1.4

9.3 Code for Document Functions

Document code is placed in *TicTacToeDoc.h* and *TicTacToeDoc.cpp*.

Add data prototypes and data variables Code 901 by hand to *TicTacToeDoc.h* under // *Operations*.

Code 901 Prototypes and Variables

```
void      CheckForGameOver ();
int       GetRectID (CPoint point);
int       IsWinner ();
BOOL      IsDraw ();
void      ResetGame ();

int m_nGameGrid[9];            // the data -- X and O in the grid
int m_nNextChar;               // X or O is next (EX or OH)
static const CRect m_rcSquares[9];    // size and position of board squares
```

In effect we are replacing JP's *CMainwindow* with *CTicTacToeDoc*.

Add Define Code 902 after *#endif*, to the *TicTacToeDoc.cpp*.

Code 902 Define

```
#define EX 1
#define OH 2
```

Add all of the following data functions to *TicTacToeDoc.cpp*

Code 903 IsWinner

```
int CTicTacToeDoc::IsWinner ()
{
    static int nPattern[8][3] = {
        0, 1, 2,
        3, 4, 5,
        6, 7, 8,
        0, 3, 6,
        1, 4, 7,
        2, 5, 8,
        0, 4, 8,
        2, 4, 6
    };

    for (int i=0; i<8; i++) {
        if ((m_nGameGrid[nPattern[i][0]] == EX) &&
            (m_nGameGrid[nPattern[i][1]] == EX) &&
            (m_nGameGrid[nPattern[i][2]] == EX))
            return EX;

        if ((m_nGameGrid[nPattern[i][0]] == OH) &&
            (m_nGameGrid[nPattern[i][1]] == OH) &&
            (m_nGameGrid[nPattern[i][2]] == OH))
            return OH;
    }
    return 0;
}
```

IsWinner () returns an EX if X wins, an OH if O wins, or a zero if neither player wins. Consequently the *if* expression (*nWinner* = *IsWinner ()*) assigns an EX, OH, or zero to variable nWinner.

Array The general form of a single dimension array is *type name[size]*. The *static* modifier, as in *static type name[size]*, creates permanent storage for the array. This means the array contents are preserved between function calls. The contents are always available.

Static *static int nPattern[8][3]* is declared here. It is a two dimensional array of 24 numbers arranged as 8 rows of 3 numbers per row, which are initalized as shown. Each array row represents a winner of 3 X's or 3 O's. Each array element is the number of a board square. The numbers 0 to 8 are the numbers of the 9 squares in the Tic Tac Toe game board.

Reading an array The array *nPattern[ ]* stores winner sequences of X's and O's. For example the 3 square numbers 2, 4, 6 in *nPattern[ ]* row 7 represents a winner, because squares 2, 4, 6 are a diagonal of board squares.

If a player marks squares 2, 4, 6 with an X, then *m_nGameGrid* elements 2, 4, 6 are set to 1. {The array *m_nGameGrid[9]* stores the X's and O's selected by the players.) Ascertaining whether or not there is a winner requires reading arrays *nPattern and m_nGameGrid*.

For loops The for loop repeatedly reads out the values of sequences of 3 elements of array *m_nGameGrid*, and AND's the 3 values. If the AND = 1, then 3 X's or 3 O's is a winner. Each sequence is determined by the elements in a row of array *nPattern*.

The elements of *m_nGameGrid* were set to zero by the function *OnNewDocument* (page 91). Therefore an element equal to zero means a player did NOT place an X or O in the corresponding square. In turn this means the game is not over, and function *IsDraw* returns a FALSE on exit.

The game is indeed over if no element equals zero, because that means 9 X's and O's have been played. Then the *IsDraw if* statement does not execute, and instead *return TRUE* executes.

Code 904 IsDraw

```
BOOL CTicTacToeDoc::IsDraw ()
{
   for (int i=0; i<9; i++) {
     if (m_nGameGrid[i] == 0)
        return FALSE;
   }
   return TRUE;
}
```

Code 905 ResetGame

```
void CTicTacToeDoc::ResetGame ()
{
   m_nNextChar = EX;
   ::ZeroMemory (m_nGameGrid, 9 * sizeof (int));
}
```

ResetGame zeros the elements of array *m_nGameGrid*. To know why see function *IsDraw* above. *ZeroMemory* is an MFC function.

Code 906 CheckForGameOver

```
// If the grid contains 3 consecutive Xs or Os, declare a winner & Start a new
// game.
// Else if the grid is full, declare a draw and start a new game.

void CTicTacToeDoc::CheckForGameOver ()
{
   int nWinner;
   if (nWinner = IsWinner ()) {
     CString string = (nWinner == EX)
                ? _T ("X wins! Game Over") : _T ("O wins! Game Over");
     AfxMessageBox (string, MB_ICONEXCLAMATION | MB_OK, 0);
     ResetGame ();
   }
   else if (IsDraw ()) {
     AfxMessageBox
     (_T ("It's a draw! Game Over"), MB_ICONEXCLAMATION | MB_OK, 0);
     ResetGame ();
   }
}
```

Variable CString string is assigned the 0 or 1 stored in *nWinner*.

? operator The ? operator takes the general form *Exp1 ? Exp2 : Exp3*. If Exp1 is true, then Exp2 is evaluated. If Exp1 is false, then Exp3 is evaluated.
Exp1 is *CString string = (nWinner == EX)*, which evaluates to 0 or 1.

Code 907 Define the board squares.

```
const CRect CTicTacToeDoc::m_rcSquares[9] = {
    CRect ( 16,  16, 112, 112),
    CRect (128,  16, 224, 112),
    CRect (240,  16, 336, 112),
    CRect ( 16, 128, 112, 224),
    CRect (128, 128, 224, 224),
    CRect (240, 128, 336, 224),
    CRect ( 16, 240, 112, 336),
    CRect (128, 240, 224, 336),
    CRect (240, 240, 336, 336)
};
```

Define the board squares as 9 rectangles in array *m_rcSquares[9]*.

Code 908 GetRectID

```
// Test each of the grid's nine squares for an X or O, and return a rectangle
// integer ID (0 to 8) if  mouse (point.x, point.y) lies inside a square (rectangle)

int CTicTacToeDoc::GetRectID (CPoint point)
{
    for (int i=0; i<9; i++) {
        if (m_rcSquares[i].PtInRect (point))
            return i;
    }
    return -1;
}
```

CRect::PtInRect is an MFC member function of class *CRect*.

Function *BOOL PtInRect(POINT point) const* return value is nonzero if the point lies within any board array square, otherwise return value is **0**.

Array *m_rcSquares[9]* is defined as *static const CRect m_rcSquares[9]*.

Therefore *m_rcSquares[9]* can dot execute the *CRECT* member function *PtInRect* as in *m_rcSquares[i].PtInRect (point)*, which returns a 1 if a mouse click is in square i.

A return of 1 means *return i* is executed (mouse click is in a square). A return of 0 means *return –1* is executed (click is not in a square).

Initialize data via *CTicTacToeDoc::OnNewDocument( )*. The data is stored in the array *m_nGameGrid[9]* where a 1 (one) represents an X (EX) and a 0 (zero) represents an O (OH). Initialize *m_nGameGrid[9]* by filing it with zeros.

Code 909 OnNewDocument

```
BOOL CTicTacToeDoc::OnNewDocument()
{
  if (!CDocument::OnNewDocument())
    return FALSE;
  // (SDI documents will reuse this document)
  ::ZeroMemory (m_nGameGrid, 9 * sizeof (int));
  m_nNextChar = EX;     // start with X

  return TRUE;
}
```

Data is initialized via *CTicTacToeDoc::OnNewDocument( )*.

MFC function *ZeroMemory* stores zeros in all elements of array *m_nGameGrid[9]*.

The game will start with the player who uses X, because variable *m_nNextChar = EX*.

As the game is played the X and O data is stored in the array *m_nGameGrid[9]* where a 1 (one) represents an X (EX) and a 0 (zero) represents an O (OH).

9.4 Code for View Functions

View code is placed in *TicTacToeView.h* and *TicTacToeView.cpp*

The view accesses document code via the *GetDocument* function (page 91) by creating the pointer *pDoc*. Data read and write are enabled when the following code line is added to View functions.

CTicTacToeDoc* pDoc = GetDocument();

> Use *pDoc* –> in View functions to read data from, and write data to, any document.

Examples: (note addition of *View* to names fetching data)
1) READ
m_nNextChar returns integer 0 or 1, which is assigned to *m_nNextCharView*. In turn the integer is used in subsequent code lines.

```
int m_nNextCharView = pDoc –> m_nNextChar;   // get data
if (m_nNextCharView != EX)
return;
```

2) READ
GetRectID returns an integer, which is assigned to *GetRectIDView*. In turn the integer is assigned to *nPos*, which is used in subsequent code lines.

```
int GetRectIDView = pDoc –> GetRectID (point);
int nPos = GetRectIDView;
```

3) READ
nPos is used in following code lines such as this one.

```
int m_nGameGridView = pDoc –> m_nGameGrid[nPos] ;
if ((nPos == –1) || (m_nGameGridView != 0))
return;
```

4) WRITE
Add an X to the game grid and set *m_nNextChar* to OH.
```
pDoc –> m_nGameGrid[nPos] = EX;
pDoc –> m_nNextChar = OH;
```

9.4.1 Code for Drawing on the Screen

The Tic Tac Toe board is defined by data array m_rcSquares[9].

We need to know where to draw an X or an O. This is why we need the number of the square a player clicked the mouse in.

The data function *GetRectID* returns the number of that square (0 to 8). The function returns a –1 if the mouse was not clicked on a square. A data read fetches the number of the 'clicked' square.

The view functions *DrawX* and *DrawO* simply draw an X or an O.

The view function *DrawBoard* draws the 9 square grid and any X's or O's that players may have entered.

The data array *m_nGameGrid[i]* contains the players' X and O information.

Add these two lines before the corresponding message handler lines in *TicTacToeView.cpp*.

```
/////////////////////////////////////////////////////////////////////////////
// CTicTacToeView support functions
```

Add prototypes by hand under // *operations public* in *TicTacToeView.h*.
Code 910 Prototypes

```
void DrawX (CDC* pDC, int nPos);
void DrawO (CDC* pDC, int nPos);
void DrawBoard (CDC* pDC);
```

Add defines by hand after *#endif*, to the *TicTacToeView.cpp*.
Code 911 Defines

```
#define EX 1
#define OH 2
```

Add functions by hand to *TicTacToeView.cpp* under support functions.

Code 912 DrawX

```
void CTicTacToeView::DrawX (CDC* pDC, int nPos)
{
    CTicTacToeDoc* pDoc = GetDocument ();

    CRect m_rcSquaresView = pDoc -> m_rcSquares[nPos];  // get data

    CPen pen (PS_SOLID, 10, RGB (255, 0, 0));
    CPen* pOldPen = pDC -> SelectObject (&pen);

    CRect rect = m_rcSquaresView;
    rect.DeflateRect (16, 16);
    pDC -> MoveTo (rect.left, rect.top);
    pDC -> LineTo (rect.right, rect.bottom);
    pDC -> MoveTo (rect.left, rect.bottom);
    pDC -> LineTo (rect.right, rect.top);

    pDC -> SelectObject (pOldPen);
}
```

nPos The number of the square in which an X is to be drawn is stored in variable *nPos*.

Arrow operator pDC is a device context pointer [JP39]. A pointer accesses device context functions by using the arrow operator –>.

Code 913 DrawO

```
void CTicTacToeView::DrawO (CDC* pDC, int nPos)
{
    CTicTacToeDoc* pDoc = GetDocument ();
      CRect m_rcSquaresView = pDoc -> m_rcSquares[nPos];     // get data
    CPen pen (PS_SOLID, 10, RGB (0, 0, 255));
    CPen* pOldPen = pDC -> SelectObject (&pen);
    pDC -> SelectStockObject (NULL_BRUSH);

    CRect rect = m_rcSquaresView;
    rect.DeflateRect (16, 16);
    pDC -> Ellipse (rect);
    pDC -> SelectObject (pOldPen);
}
```

nPos The number of the square in which an O is to be drawn is stored in variable *nPos*.

SelectStockObject( ) is an MFC function [JP73].

The NULL_BRUSH parameter means the brush draws nothing [JP74] so that the background color is white in this case.

Code 914 DrawBoard

```
void CTicTacToeView::DrawBoard (CDC* pDC)
{
    // Draw the lines that define the tic-tac-toe grid.
    CPen pen (PS_SOLID, 10, RGB (0, 0, 0));
    CPen* pOldPen = pDC ->SelectObject (&pen);
      pDC -> MoveTo (120, 16);
      pDC -> LineTo (120, 336);
    pDC -> MoveTo (232, 16);
    pDC -> LineTo (232, 336);
      pDC -> MoveTo (16, 120);
      pDC -> LineTo (336, 120);
    pDC -> MoveTo (16, 232);
    pDC -> LineTo (336, 232);

    // Draw the Xs and Os players have entered.
    CTicTacToeDoc* pDoc = GetDocument ();
    for (int i=0; i<9; i++) {
      int m_nGameGridView = pDoc -> m_nGameGrid[i];   // get data

      if (m_nGameGridView == EX)
        DrawX (pDC, i);
      else if (m_nGameGridView == OH)
        DrawO (pDC, i);
    }
    pDC ->SelectObject (pOldPen);
}
```

Code 915 Add to *OnDraw*

```
DrawBoard (pDC);
pDC -> TextOut (400, 100, CString (_T ("For help click on HELP menu
item")));
```

Programming with MFC

9.4.2 Code for Mouse Events and Message Handlers

Click on *View*, click on *ClassWizard*, click on *Message Maps*.
Check project is *TicTacToe*, class name is *CTicTacToeView*.
In the *Object Ids* box click on *CTicTacToeView*
In the *Messages* box click on *WM_LButtonDblClk*.
Click on *Add Function* to add *OnLButtonDblClk*.
Click on *Edit Code* to see function added as a skeleton message handler.

These actions add code items 1, 2, 3.

1) to *TicTacToeView.h* a prototype function
    afx_msg void OnLButtonDblClk(UINT nFlags, CPoint point);

2) to the message map in *TicTacToeView.cpp* the function
    ON_WM_LBUTTONDBLCLK( ).

3) in *TicTacToeView.cpp* a skeleton message handler
void CTicTacToeView::OnLButtonDblClk(UINT nFlags, CPoint point)

Repeat for *WM_LBUTTONDOWN and WM_ RBUTTONDOWN.*

Add Code 916 to *TicTacToeView.cpp* under message handlers
Code 916 OnLButtonDblClk

```
void CTicTacToeView::OnLButtonDblClk(UINT nFlags, CPoint point)
{
    // TODO: Add your message handler code here and/or call default
    // Reset the game if one of the thick black lines defining the game
    // grid is double-clicked with the left mouse button.

    CTicTacToeDoc* pDoc = GetDocument ( );

    CDC* pDC = GetDC ( );
    if (pDC -> GetPixel (point) == RGB (0, 0, 0))     // reset if black pixel
    {   pDoc -> ResetGame ( );
        Invalidate ( );
    }
    ReleaseDC (pDC);
    CView::OnLButtonDblClk(nFlags, point);
}
```

Use F1 to fetch this information used in *OnLButtonDblClk*.
CDC::GetPixel
COLORREF GetPixel(int *x*, int *y*) const;
COLORREF GetPixel(POINT *point*) const

GetPixel retrieves the RGB color value of the pixel at the point specified
by *x* and *y*. The point must be in the clipping region. If the point is not in
the clipping region the function has no effect and returns −1.

Code 917 OnLButtonDown

```
void CTicTacToeView::OnLButtonDown(UINT nFlags, CPoint point)
{
    // TODO: Add your message handler code here and/or call default
    // Do nothing if it's O's turn, if the click occurred outside the
    // tic-tac-toe grid, or if a nonempty square was clicked.

    CTicTacToeDoc* pDoc = GetDocument ();

    int m_nNextCharView = pDoc -> m_nNextChar;   // get data
    if (m_nNextCharView != EX)
    return;

    int GetRectIDView = pDoc -> GetRectID (point);
    int nPos = GetRectIDView;
    int m_nGameGridView = pDoc -> m_nGameGrid[nPos];
    if ((nPos == -1) || (m_nGameGridView != 0))
    return;

    // Add an X to the game grid and toggle m_nNextChar.
    pDoc -> m_nGameGrid[nPos] = EX;
    pDoc -> m_nNextChar = OH;

    // Draw an X on the screen and see if either player has won.

    CDC* pDC = GetDC ();
    DrawX (pDC, nPos);
    ReleaseDC (pDC);

    pDoc -> CheckForGameOver ();

    CView::OnLButtonDown(nFlags, point);
}
```

Programming with MFC

Code 918 OnRButtonDown

```
void CTicTacToeView::OnRButtonDown(UINT nFlags, CPoint point)
{
    // Do nothing if it's X's turn, if the click occurred outside the
    // tic-tac-toe grid, or if a nonempty square was clicked.

    CTicTacToeDoc* pDoc = GetDocument ();

    int m_nNextCharView = pDoc -> m_nNextChar;   // get data
    if (m_nNextCharView != OH)
    return;

    int GetRectIDView = pDoc -> GetRectID (point);
    int nPos = GetRectIDView;
    int m_nGameGridView = pDoc -> m_nGameGrid[nPos];
    if ((nPos == -1) || (m_nGameGridView != 0))
     return;

    // Add an O to the game grid and toggle m_nNextChar.
    pDoc -> m_nGameGrid[nPos] = OH;
    pDoc -> m_nNextChar = EX;

    // Draw an O on the screen and see if either player has won.
    CDC* pDC = GetDC ();
    DrawO (pDC, nPos);
    ReleaseDC (pDC);

    pDoc -> CheckForGameOver ();

    CView::OnRButtonDown(nFlags, point);
}
```

9.5 Code for Menu Items

The menus listed across the top of the TicTacToe window are in the *top-level* menu. Clicking on a menu produces a *drop-down* menu consisting of a list of one or more *menu items*. The intent here is to add a *HELP* menu item, and a *Reset* menu item (as an alternative to left button double clicking),

1) Click *ResourceView* pane. Click on +TicTacToe resources. Click on +*Menu*, double click on *IDR_MAINFRAME*.

98

2) In the menu bar, right click on *File* menu item *New*. Right click on *Properties*.

   change the ID to *ID_FILE_RESET*

   change the caption to *&Reset\tCtrl+R*

   click on X.

3) Create a message handler for the *Reset* menu item.

In the *View* menu click on *ClassWizard* to open *MFC ClassWizard*.

   Set Project to *TicTacToe*, classname to *CTicTacToeView*.

   In Object IDs click on *ID_FILE_RESET*.

   In Messages click on *COMMAND*.

   Click on *Add Function* button.

   OnFileReset appears in the Add Member Functions box.

   Click on OK.

   Click on Edit code button to get *CTicTacToeView::OnFileReset*.

Verify that *afx_msg void OnFileReset(); is in TicTacToeView.h.*

Verify *ON_COMMAND(ID_FILE_RESET, OnFileReset)* is in the *TicTacToeView.cpp* message map.

Code 919 OnFileReset - Add to *TicTacToeView.cpp*.

```
void CTicTacToeView::OnFileReset()
{
    CTicTacToeDoc* pDoc = GetDocument ();
    CDC* pDC = GetDC ();
    {
        pDoc  –> ResetGame ();
        Invalidate ( );
    }
    ReleaseDC (pDC);
}
```

4) In the *ReseouceView IDR_MAINFRAME* menu bar, click on *Help* to see the drop down menu items. Click on the blank menu item. Right click on *Properties*.

   change the ID to *ID_HELP1* (to avoid conflict with Visual help)

   change the caption to *&Help*

   click on X

Programming with MFC

5) Create a message handler for the *HELP* menu item.

In the C++ *View* menu click on *Class Wizard* to open *MFC Class Wizard*.
  Set Project to *TicTacToe*, classname to *CTicTacToeView*.
  In Object IDs click on *ID_HELP1*.
  In Messages click on *COMMAND*.
  Click on *Add Function* button.
  OnHelp1 appears in the Add Member Functions box.
  Click on OK.
  Click on Edit code button to get *CMainFrame::OnHelp1*

Verify that *afx_msg void OnHelp1( );* is in *TicTacToeView.h*.

Verify that *ON_COMMAND(ID_HELP, OnHelp1)* is in the
TicTacToeView.cpp message map.

Add Code 920 to *TicTacToeView.cpp*.

Code 920 OnHelp1

```
void CMainFrame::OnHelp1( )
{
    // TODO: Add your command handler code here
    CString strHELP;

    strHELP = (CString)
    "Left button click on a square to enter an X."
    + "\n"
    + "Right button click on a square to enter an O."
    + "\n"
    + "Left button double click on a grid line to clear the board and start a new
game."
    + "\n"
    + "Click menu item RESET to clear the board and start a new game."
    + "\n"
    ;
    AfxMessageBox (strHELP, MB_ICONEXCLAMATION | MB_OK, 0);
}
```

10 Design a Wizard

This design project shows how to create a wizard. One dialog box for each wizard property page is added to the project.

10.1 Create the *Wizard* Workspace

Follow the procedure in Chapter 1 Section 1.3 for *Dialog Based* except as follows.

Type the name *Wizard* in the *Project Name* edit box.
Note addition of *Wizard* in the *Location* edit box.

10.2 Build the *Wizard* Project

Follow the procedure in Chapter 1, Section 1.4.

Note: After adding code to any file repeat 10.2 to check for errors.

Figure 1001 Wizard

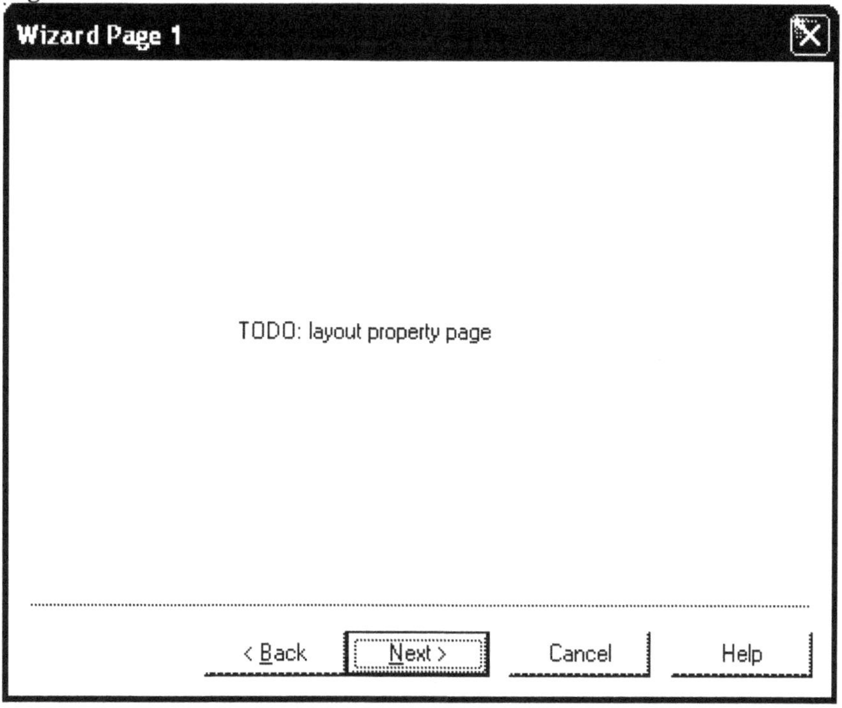

10.3 Use *ResourceView* to create Four Property Pages

1 Click *ResourceView* Tab in left pane.
  Click *+Wizard Resources.*
  Click *+Dialog.*
  Double click on IDD_WIZARD_DIALOG

2 Click *Insert* in menu bar at top of screen,
  Click *Resource*
  Click on *+Dialog* in *Insert Resource* dialog box.
  Click on *IDD_Proppage_Large.*
  Click on *New.*
  IDD_PROPPAGE_LARGE appears, and the *Property Page* dialog box
  appears in right pane.

3 Right click in the *Property Page* dialog box. Click on *Properties* to get
the *Dialog Properties* box (Figure 1002)

Figure 1002 Wizard Page 1 Properties

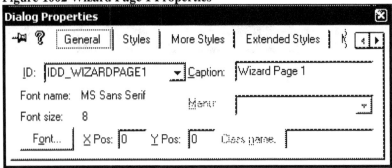

  Change ID box IDD_PROPPAGE_LARGE to IDD_WIZARDPAGE1
  Change caption box to *Wizard Page 1.*
  Click on the Styles Tab – select Style *child* and Border *dialog frame.*
  Click on X.

4 Repeat 2 and 3 for *Wizard Pages 2, 3, 4.*

10.4 Use *ClassWizard* to create four pairs of Wizard Page files

1 In the *ResourceView* Pane click on +Dialog

2 Important: double click on IDD_WIZARDPAGE1

3 In the *View* menu click *ClassWizard*.
  Click OK in the *Adding a Class* dialog *box*.
  Type *CWizardPage1* in the Name edit box
  Select *CPropertyPage* in the Base Class edit box.
  Verify Dialog ID box contains IDD_WIZARDPAGE1.
  Click on *OK*.
  Click on *OK*.
  In FileView to see new files WizardPage1.h and WizardPage1.cpp.

4 Repeat 2, 3 for *CWizardPage2, 3, 4* to create 3 more pairs of files.

10.5 Use *ClassWizard* to create a Property Sheet

1 In the *View* menu click on *ClassWizard*.
  Select the *Message Maps* tab.
  Verify project is *Wizard* and class name is *CWizardDlg* [JP449].

2 Click on *Add Class, and click on New* to open *New Class* dialog box.
  Type *CWizardPropertySheet* in the Name edit box.
  Select *CPropertySheet* in the Base Class edit box.
  Click on *OK*.   Click on *OK* to close *ClassWizard*.
  In Fileview see new files *WizardPropertySheet.h* and *.cpp*.

3 Add code to *WizardPropertySheet.h*.
Add Code 1001 below the line *// WizardPropertySheet.h : header file*.
Code 1001

```
#include "WizardPage1.h"
#include "WizardPage2.h"
#include "WizardPage3.h"
#include "WizardPage4.h"
```

Add Code 1002 after *DECLARE_DYNAMIC(CAcquirePropertySheet)*.
Code 1002

```
public:
CWizardPage1 m_WizardPage1;
CWizardPage2 m_WizardPage2;
CWizardPage3 m_WizardPage3;
CWizardPage4 m_WizardPage4;
```

4 Add code to *WizardPropertySheet.cpp*.
Add Code 1003 to the *FIRST* 2, repeat 2, constructors.
Code 1003

```
AddPage(&m_WizardPage1);
AddPage(&m_WizardPage2);
AddPage(&m_WizardPage3);
AddPage(&m_WizardPage4);
```

5 Verify that the following code is in *WizardPropertySheet.cpp*
   #include " WizardPropertySheet.h"

6 In *WizardDlg.cpp* add *#include "WizardPropertySheet.h"* at the top of
the file.

10.6 Add Wizard Code

In CWizardDlg add Code 1004 to BOOL CWizardDlg::OnInitDialog()
Code 1004 OnInitDialog

```
BOOL CWizardDlg::OnInitDialog()
{
  CDialog::OnInitDialog();
  // Set the icon for this dialog.  The framework does this automatically
  //  when the application's main window is not a dialog
  SetIcon(m_hIcon, TRUE);     // Set big icon
  SetIcon(m_hIcon, FALSE);    // Set small icon

  // TODO: Add extra initialization here
  CWizardPropertySheet propsh(_T("Wizard Property Sheet Design"));
  propsh.SetWizardMode();
  propsh.DoModal();
  return TRUE; // return TRUE  unless you set the focus to a control
}
```

11 ADD - a Task Project

This *task project* produces the ADD program that takes a user through the series of steps required to execute the task, which is the addition of two integers according to the *Standard Addition Algorithm with Carry* (see the sidebar on page 106).

The *ADD* Program Design

There are two program phases: *setup the problem* and *do the problem*.

The *setup the problem* phase is drawn on the screen by *OnDraw*. The user responds to requests with key presses processed by *OnChar* that setup the problem. A yes response to the y, n request for a key press starts the *do the problem* mode, which is then drawn on the screen by *OnDraw*. A no response starts over.

OnDraw and *OnChar* each have two parts. The first part is devoted to *setup the problem* and the second part to *do the problem*.

By design the only active keys are Enter, Backspace, q, Q, y, Y, n, N, and 0 to 9.

The programs are developed with the aid of Visual C++ 6.0. Program filenames are generated by Visual C++ 6.0. Code is added only to *AddView.h*, *AddView.cpp*, and resource files. There are no data files in this document/view workspace.

> Create the ADD workspace and build the ADD skeleton project per Chapter 1 Sections 1.1 and 1.4.

Program design for the windows environment is based on responding to messages generated within the program. The program takes action only in response to a message created by a key press or mouse click.

Keyboard key presses and mouse button clicks generate the action messages for the arithmetic program steps. The action messages change the values of variables so that the program moves on to the next step.

Standard Addition Algorithm with Carry (Add 56913 to 60388)

Step 1: Execute a one digit addition-with-carry in position 0.

Add the units 8+3 = 11 = 1×10 + 1
Enter the unit's 1 in answer position 0, and the ten's 1 in carry position 1.

```
    1
 60388
+ 56913
 ──────
      1
```

Step 2: Execute a one digit addition-with-carry in position 1.

Add the tens 1+8+1 = 10 = 1×10 + 0
Enter the unit's 0 in answer position 1, and the ten's 1 in carry position 2.

```
   11
 60388
+ 56913
 ──────
     01
```

Step 3: Execute a one digit addition-with-carry in position 2.

Add the hundreds 1+3+9 = 13 = 1×10 + 3
Enter the unit's 3 in answer position 2, and the ten's 1 in carry position 3.

```
  111
 60388
+ 56913
 ──────
    301
```

Step 4: Execute a one digit addition-with-carry in position 3.

Add the thousands 1+0+6 = 07 = 0×10 + 7
Enter the unit's 7 in answer position 3, and the ten's 0 in carry position 4.

```
 0111
 60388
+ 56913
 ──────
   7301
```

Step 5: Execute a one digit addition-with-carry in position 4.

Add the ten thousands 0+6+5 = 11 = 1×10 + 1
Enter the unit's 1 in answer position 4, and the ten's 1 in carry position 5.

```
10111
 60388
+ 56913
 ──────
  17301
```

Step 6: Execute a one digit addition-with-carry in position 5.

Add the hundred thousands 1+0+0 = 01 = 0×10 + 1
Enter the unit's 1 in answer position 5, and the ten's 0 in carry position 6 (not shown). Since the carry is 0 we are done.

```
10111
 60388
+ 56913
 ──────
 117301
```

Events move the ADD program along.

The *windows message process* is very different from a conventional program executing instructions sequentially, requesting user responses, and responding to responses.

Windows programs are driven by events. In this program events are a user clicking a mouse button, or a user pressing a key. The *ADD* program responds to each event by issuing a windows message, which is placed in the window's message queue. The message queue is accessed by the *ADD* program's message handler functions such as *OnChar*. In this way events are translated into actions.

Understanding what follows requires that this difference is kept in mind.

Messages to user direct the user.

Part 1: set up the problem (variable *m_nstart* = 0)

1 "Select number of digits (d1 = 2 to 5) in first number:"
    User responds by entering digit d1 and pressing enter.

2 "Select number of digits (d2 = 2 to 5) in second number:"
    User responds by entering digit d2 and pressing enter.

3 "Ready to do problems (yes, no)?:"
    User responds by entering y or n and pressing enter. A yes moves the program on *to do* the problem. A no returns to step 1.

A random number generator produces numbers n1 and n2 with corresponding number of digits d1 and d2, which are printed on the screen.

Part 2: do the problem (variable *m_nstart* = 1)

A *caret* that moves along marks slots where the user is supposed to enter digits as the solution process progresses.

Fill in the slots (do the problem). After each problem slot is filled with a digit, or passed over, the control variable *m_ni* is set to 1.

Then, depending on the user's "solution" to the problem, one of the following messages is displayed in a message dialog box. The messages require a yes or no answer.

Case 1
IF statement "Correct! Do a new problem?"
  Yes sets up a new problem with new n1 and n2.
  No increments case variable *m_ni* to 1.

ELSE statement "Not correct. Try it again?"
  Yes sets up the same problem with same n1 and n2.
  No increments *m_ni* to 2.

Case 2: do a new problem if not correct?
  Yes sets up a new problem with same d1 and d2.
  No increments *m_ni* to 3.

Case 3: change number of digits or quit (m_ni=3)
  Yes quits the program.
  No returns to part 1 so that user can start over.

Figure 1101 Set up the Problem

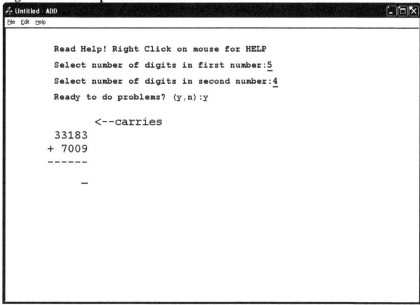

```
 Untitled - ADD                                        _ □ X
File  Edit  Help

        Read Help! Right Click on mouse for HELP
        Select number of digits in first number:5
        Select number of digits in second number:4
        Ready to do problems? (y,n):y

               <--carries
         33183
        + 7009
        ------
               _
```

Figure 1102 Do the Problem

```
 Untitled - ADD                                        _ □ X
File  Edit  Help




         11110  <--carries
          47583
         +86751
         ------
         134334
           _
```

11.1 Setup and Do Skeleton Structure

Variables control progress through the *ADD* program. Variables implement the logic of the program. Variable *m_nStart* selects the *setup* mode or the *do* mode.

Program design The design divides into two parts: *setup the problem* (*m_nStart* = 0) and *do the problem* (*m_nStart* = 1). The design starts by using the function *OnDraw* to draw on the screen the *setup the problem* questions the user is asked to answer (how many digits in each of the two numbers to be added and do you want to do the problem). A yes answer switches to the *do the problem* mode producing two random numbers, with the selected number of digits, and drawing the problem on the screen. The user then does the problem by entering digits in slots.

OnChar also has two parts that process the user's key press responses during *setup the problem(m_nStart=0)* and *do the problem(m_nStart=1)*.

OnDraw The *OnDraw* function (in *ADDview.cpp*) draws on the screen the current status of the problem the user is solving. E.g. partial digit sums and carries are drawn immediately after a digit entry by the user. *OnDraw* does not change the value of any variables. The functions in *OnChar* enter (solution) digits and change variable values in response to key presses. The responses to any key differ according to the modes *setup* or *do*. The *OnDraw* set up and do structure has two parts, marked as A1 and A2, which are activated according to the value of variable *m_nStart* (Code 1101). The skeletons are filled in as we proceed.

Code 1101 *OnDraw* set up and do structure – add code to *ADDView.cpp*

```
int m_nStart;       // add to ADDView.h Implementation public
void CAddView::OnDraw(CDC* pDC)
{
    if (m_nStart==0)      //  A1
    {
        // setup the problem
    }
    if (m_nStart==1)       //  A2
    {
        // display and do the problem
    }
}   //end of OnDraw
```

Add OnChar for Message Passing Click on View, click on Class Wizard, click on Message Maps.

Figure 1103 Shows that WM_CHAR message has been added

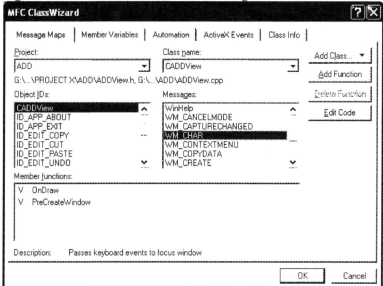

Verify Project is *ADD*, Class is *CADDView* (Figure 1103).
In the *Object IDs* box click on *CADDView*.
In the *Messages* box click on *WM_CHAR*..
This activates the *Add Function* button.
Click on *Add Function* to add *OnChar* to *ADDView.cpp*.
Click on edit code to see the *OnChar* function.
Click on OK. This adds code items 1, 2, 3.

1) to *ADDView.h* a prototype function
afx_msg void OnChar(UINT nChar, UINT nRepCnt, UINT nFlags);
2) to the message map in *ADDView.cpp* the function
ON_WM_CHAR()
3) in *ADDView.cpp* a skeleton message handler.
void CADDView::OnChar(UINT nChar, UINT nRepCnt, UINT nFlags)

>> Repeat this process. This time in the *Messages* box click on *OnInitialUpdate*. This process adds code items 1 and 3 (no 2).
1) *virtual void OnInitialUpdate();*
3) *void CADDView::OnInitialUpdate()*

OnChar In the *ADD* program *OnChar* (in *ADDView.cpp*) uses the switch function. The switch function in B1 (Codes 1102, 1103) defines key press responses that setup the problem. The switch function in B2 defines key press responses that do the problem. Each switch function *case* defines an active key (Enter, Backspace, Y, N, Q, y, n, q, 0 to 9). Associated with each case are statements defining the key press actions. *OnChar* changes the value of variables to move the program along.

The last code line in the *OnChar* IF and ELSE statements is the *Invalidate* function, which calls *OnDraw* to redraw the screen. A key press takes us back to *OnChar*. This is how program goes to and from *OnChar* and *OnDraw*.

OnChar is written with an *if-else* statement. To show the difference, we wrote *OnDraw* with two *if* statements, which we prefer.

All key presses are processed by message handlers in *OnChar*.

Consequently
1) each key press generates a *WM_CHAR* message that calls the *OnChar* function,

2) the switch *case* corresponding to the key pressed is executed,

3) *Invalidate* calls *OnDraw* to draw on the screen the current status of the problem the user is processing. The screen is redrawn after each key press to reflect changes implemented by each key press.

Code 1102 OnChar Set up and Do Structure – add code to *ADDView.cpp*

```
void CAddView::OnChar(UINT nChar, UINT nRepCnt, UINT nFlags)
{
  if (m_nStart==0)      //  B1
  {
     // setup the problem
  }
  else     // m_nStart==1    //  B2
  {
     // display and do the problem
  }
}
```

11.2 Skeleton for Set Up and Do the Problem

In *OnDraw*, variable *m_nDigit* selects the requests presented to the user (Code 1103). Observe the *greater than* in *m_nDigit >= 1*. User responds to each request with key presses, which are processed. Then user presses Enter. The Enter key press sends a message to *OnChar* whose switch function selects case VK_RETURN (11.9, page 124), which increments *m_nDigit*, performs other tasks, executes *Invalidate(FALSE)* to return to *OnDraw*, which redraws the screen, and moves on to the next *m_nDigit* action. Variable *m_nDigit* is incremented by 1 each time the Enter key is pressed. In this way requests are sequentially presented to the user. After the *m_nDigit == 3* statement is executed the *do the problem* mode is entered.

Code 1103 Skeleton for set up and do the problem. Add to *ADDView.cpp*.

```
int m_nDigit, m_ni;        // add to ADDView.h

void CAddView::OnDraw(CDC* pDC)
{
    if (m_nStart==0)    // setup the problem   A1
    {
        if (m_nDigit >= 1)
        {    }   //   user selects 1,2,3,4, or 5 and presses Enter

        if (m_nDigit >= 2)
        {    }   //   user selects 1,2,3,4, or 5 and presses Enter

        if (m_nDigit == 3)
        {    }   //   user selects y or n and presses Enter   (y sets m_nStart = 1)
    }  //end of m_nStart==0 setup
    if (m_nStart==1)    // display and do the problem   A2
    {
        // code here that displays the problem on the screen for user to do
        switch(m_ni)   //process message box responses
        {
            case 1:        // select correct/not correct
            break;
            case 2:        // select do a new problem if not correct?
            break;
            case 3:        // change number of digits or quit
            break;
        }
    }  //end of m_nStart==1
} //end of OnDraw
```

11.3 The Caret and the Font

The *caret* is the flashing horizontal (or vertical) bar used by applications to mark the point (aka slot) on the screen where the next text character will be inserted when a key is pressed [JP154].

A key press creates a keyboard message. Keyboard messages are sent to the window that has the "input focus" [JP144]. The "input focus" message names are WM_SETFOCUS and WM_KILLFOCUS. The associated functions are OnSetFocus and OnKillfocus. These two functions are used to create and destroy the caret as focus is gained and lost by a window. Class Wizard facilitates adding these two functions.

Click on View, click on Class Wizard, click on Message Maps.

Figure 1104 Shows that WM_KILLFOCUS message has been added

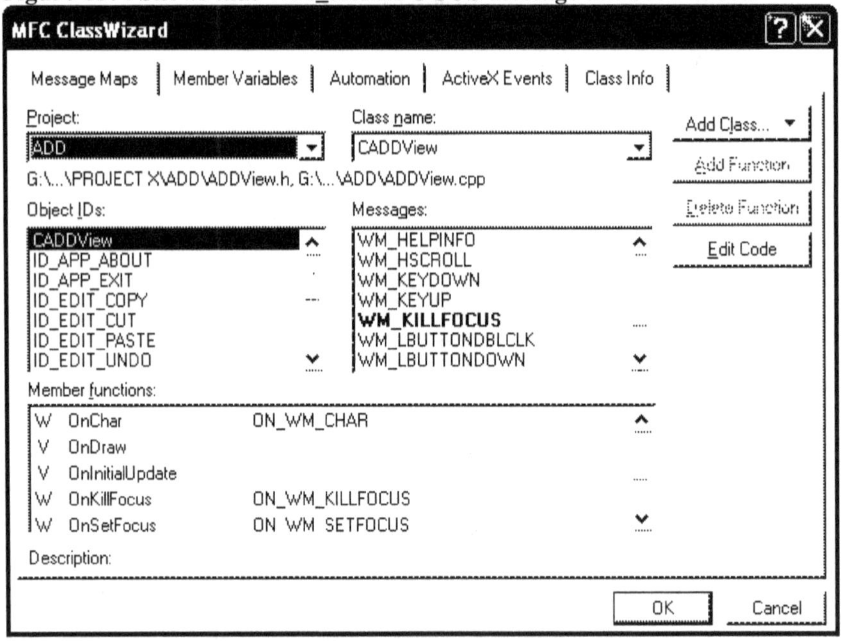

Verify Project is *ADD*, Class is *CADDView* (Figure 1104).
In the *Object IDs* box click on *CADDView*.
In the *Messages* box choices appear. Click *WM_KILLFOCUS*.
This activates the *Add Function* button.
Click on *Add Function* to add *OnKillFocus* to *ADDView.cpp*.
Click on edit code to see the *OnKillFocus* function.

Click on OK. This adds code items 1, 2, 3.

1) to *ADDView.h* a prototype function
afx_msg void OnKillFocus(CWnd* pNewWnd);

2) to the message map in *ADDView.cpp* the function
ON_WM_KILLFOCUS()

3) in *ADDView.cpp* a skeleton message handler.
void CADDView::OnKillFocus(CWnd* pNewWnd)

>>> Repeat this process to add *OnSetFocus*.

Code 1104 add to *ADDView.h*

```
CPoint  m_ptCaretPos;
int   m_nxChar, m_nyChar;        // also used by font function
```

Code 1105 add to *ADDView.cpp*

```
void CAddView::OnKillFocus(CWnd* pNewWnd)
{
  CView::OnKillFocus(pNewWnd);

  // TODO: Add your message handler code here
  HideCaret();
  m_ptCaretPos = GetCaretPos();
  ::DestroyCaret();
}
```

Code 1106 add to*ADDView.cpp*

```
void CAddView::OnSetFocus(CWnd* pOldWnd)
{
  CView::OnSetFocus(pOldWnd);

  // TODO: Add your message handler code here
  CreateSolidCaret(m_nxChar,max(2,::GetSystemMetrics(SM_CYBORDER)));
  SetCaretPos(m_ptCaretPos);
  ShowCaret();
}
```

Programming with MFC

We desire different font point heights for setup the problem and do the problem. The program uses two font sizes; one for requesting user input to setup the problem (TEXTF) and another for the problem (PROBF).

Code 1107 Font defines. Add to *ADDView.cpp*.

```
#define TEXTF 14      // text font size
#define PROBF 18      // problem font size
```

This is why we created a "Courier New" font with font point height n as a parameter [JP69]. *SelectAFont(n, pDC)*, as written (Code 1109), creates a "Courier New" font with size n points. When font size is changed caret size is also changed. Add *SelectAFont* to ADDView.cpp.

Code 1108 *SelectAFont* prototype and a variable. Add to *ADDView.h*.

```
public:
  void SelectAFont(int n,CDC* pDC);
  CFont* m_pOldFont;
```

Code 1109 Font Function Add as a support function to *ADDView.cpp*

```
void CADDView::SelectAFont(int n, CDC *pDC)
{
  int nHeight = - ((pDC -> GetDeviceCaps(LOGPIXELSY) * n) / 72);

  CFont aFont;                    //create font object
  aFont.CreateFont(nHeight, 0, 0, 0,
          FW_BOLD, FALSE, FALSE, 0, DEFAULT_CHARSET,
          OUT_TT_PRECIS, CLIP_DEFAULT_PRECIS,
          DEFAULT_QUALITY, FIXED_PITCH | FF_MODERN,
          "Courier New");

  m_pOldFont = pDC -> SelectObject(&aFont);

  //get char dimensions
  TEXTMETRIC tm;
  pDC -> GetTextMetrics(&tm);
  m_nxChar = tm.tmAveCharWidth;
  m_nyChar = tm.tmHeight + tm.tmExternalLeading;
}
```

Defining the font and caret for a code block requires adding two code lines in *ADDView.cpp* after *if (m_nStart==0)*   //   *A1*

```
SelectAFont(TEXTF,pDC);
CreateSolidCaret(m_nxChar,max(2,::GetSystemMetrics(SM_CYBORDER)));
```

And adding two code lines to *ADDView.cpp* after *if (m_nStart==1)* // *A2*

```
SelectAFont(PROBF,pDC);
CreateSolidCaret(m_nxChar,max(2,::GetSystemMetrics(SM_CYBORDER)));
```

Code 1110 Skeleton for set up and do the problem. Add to *ADDView.cpp*.

```
void CAddView::OnDraw(CDC* pDC)
{
    if (m_nStart==0)    // setup the problem   A1
    {
        SelectAFont(TEXTF,pDC);
        CreateSolidCaret(m_nxChar,max(2,::GetSystemMetrics(SM_CYBORDER)));
        if (m_nDigit >= 1)
        {
            //   user selects 1,2,3,4, or 5 and presses Enter
        }
        if (m_nDigit >= 2)
        {
            //   user selects 1,2,3,4, or 5 and presses Enter
        }
        if (m_nDigit == 3)
        {
            //   user selects y or n and presses Enter   (y sets m_nStart = 1)
        }
    }    //end of m_nStart==0 setup
    if (m_nStart==1)    // display and do the problem  A2
    {
        SelectAFont(PROBF,pDC);
        CreateSolidCaret(m_nxChar,max(2,::GetSystemMetrics(SM_CYBORDER)));

        switch(m_ni)   //process message box responses
        {
            case 1:        // select correct/not correct
            break;
            case 2:        // select do a new problem if not correct?
            break;
            case 3:        // change number of digits or quit
            break;
        }
    }    //end of m_nStart==1
}  //end of OnDraw
```

11.4 User is Requested to Setup the Problem

Drawing a string, the caret, and the response:
pDC –> MoveTo(x1, y1+2*(TEXTF+2));   //move to new current position
pDC –> SetTextAlign (TA_UPDATECP);   //text box to right of position
pDC –> TextOut (0,0,"Select number of digits in first number to add: ");

MoveTo changes the current position to the given x,y coordinates.
SetTextAlign updates the current position for text (TA_UPDATECP).
TextOut prints the text that is inside the quotes.

UINT SetTextAlign(UINT *nFlags*);
nFlags specifies text-alignment flags. The flags specify the relationship between a point and a rectangle that bounds the text.

TA_RIGHT Aligns the point with the right side of a bounding rectangle.

TA_UPDATECP Updates the current x-position after each call to a text-output function. The new position is at the right side of the bounding rectangle for the text. When this flag is set, the coordinates specified in calls to the **TextOut** member function are ignored, which is why the 0, 0.

TextOut writes the string to the screen starting at the updated specified location (the x,y coordinates) using the currently selected font. Note that our TextOut uses 0, 0 for x,y coordinates because of the prior x,y update.

Writing the string moved the current text position to the end of the string. SetTextAlign updates the current position for text. It aligns this new current position with the right side of the text box. (TA_UPDATECP | TA_RIGHT). The TextOut String writes a character in the text box. Initially m_nChar1 holds a space so you only see the caret. When a key is pressed the caret is replaced by the key character.

If user presses *active* key w then char w replaces the space in m_nChar1 and the screen is redrawn with char w over the caret.

Note: until Enter is pressed user can press any active key which replaces w. The user can press any set of active keys any number of times.

The caret is repositioned whenever an x,y move occurs.

Add the *OnInitialUpdate* support function.

Click on View, click on Class Wizard, click on Message Maps.
Verify Project is *ADD*, Class is *CADDView* (Figure 1104).
In the *Object IDs* box click on *CADDView*.
In the *Messages* box click *OnInitialUpdate*.
This activates the *Add Function* button.
Click on *Add Function* to add *OnInitialUpdate* to *ADDView.cpp*.
Click on edit code to see the *OnInitialUpdate* function.
Click on OK.

Add Code 1111 to *ADDview.h.*
Code 1111 Variables
ii

```
private:
  UINT  m_nChar1, m_nChar2, m_nChar, m_nCharYN;
  CPoint m_ptCaretPos;
  int  m_nxChar, m_nyChar;

public:
int m_nStart, m_nDigit, m_ni;
```

Add Code 1112 to *OnInitialUpdate in ADDview.cpp.*
Code 1112 Initialized variables

```
m_nStart = 0;
m_nDigit = 1;
m_nChar1 = ' ';
m_nChar2 = ' ';
m_nChar = ' ';
m_nCharYN = ' ';
```

Add Code 1113 to *OnDraw* in *ADDView.cpp*
Code 1113 Defines and A1 code

```
#define MAXDIGITS 5
#define TEXTF 14    //nlp text font size
#define PROBF 18    //nlp problem font size

int x0=100,y0=200,x1=100,y1=30;

if (m_nStart==0)    // setup the problem   A1
  {
    SelectAFont(TEXTF,pDC);
    CreateSolidCaret(m_nxChar,max(2,::GetSystemMetrics(SM_CYBORDER)));
```

```
if (m_nDigit >= 1)      // step 1
{
  pDC -> MoveTo(x1,y1);
  pDC -> SetTextAlign(TA_UPDATECP);
  pDC -> TextOut(0,0,"Read Help! Right Click on mouse for HELP");

  pDC -> MoveTo(x1,y1+2*(TEXTF+2));
  pDC -> SetTextAlign(TA_UPDATECP);
  pDC -> TextOut(0,0,"Select number of digits in first number: ");

  pDC -> SetTextAlign(TA_UPDATECP | TA_RIGHT);
  pDC -> TextOut(0,0,m_nChar1);

  m_ptCaretPos = pDC -> GetCurrentPosition();
  m_ptCaretPos.y += m_nyChar;
  SetCaretPos(m_ptCaretPos);
}

if (m_nDigit >= 2)      // step 2
{
  pDC -> MoveTo(x1, y1+4*(TEXTF+2));
  pDC -> SetTextAlign(TA_UPDATECP);
  pDC -> TextOut(0,0,"Select number of digits in second number: ");

  pDC -> SetTextAlign(TA_UPDATECP | TA_RIGHT);
  pDC -> TextOut(0,0,m_nChar2);

  m_ptCaretPos = pDC -> GetCurrentPosition();
  m_ptCaretPos.y += m_nyChar;
  SetCaretPos(m_ptCaretPos);
}

if (m_nDigit == 3)      // step 3
{
  pDC->MoveTo(x1,y1+6*(TEXTF+2));
  pDC->SetTextAlign(TA_UPDATECP);
  pDC->TextOut(0,0,"Ready to do problems? (y,n): ");

  pDC->SetTextAlign(TA_UPDATECP | TA_RIGHT);
  pDC->TextOut(0,0,m_nCharYN);

  m_ptCaretPos = pDC -> GetCurrentPosition();
  m_ptCaretPos.y += m_nyChar;
  SetCaretPos(m_ptCaretPos);
}
} //end of m_nStart==0 setup if
```

11.5 Creating the Numbers to Add

Here is how the two numbers to be added are created. User is asked to select number-of-digits d1 and d2 that are *stored as characters*. If either selection is greater than 5, logic forces a change to 5. If d1 < d2 then d1 and d2 are exchanged so that d1>d2. The function *Numbers* is used to generate the integer numbers n1 and n2 with numbers of digits corresponding to d1 and d2. Here is how Numbers does that.

Numbers calculates maximum possible (long) numbers $m\_lmx1 = 10\char`^d1$ and $m\_lmx2 = 10\char`^d2$. Then the max numbers are used by RandRange to produce two (long) random numbers m_ln_1 and m_ln_2, which will be added. For example d1 = 3 then $m\_lmx1 = 1000$ and n1 is randomly select from the range 100<= n1 < 1000 so that n1 ranges from 100 to 999.

The answer to the problem is calculated so that the users' answer can be marked correct or not correct. The answer is $m\_lresult = m\_ln1 + m\_ln2$.

The digit sums and carries are placed in *slots* as the addition is implemented. The number of slots in the problem, maxslot, is calculated. For example, if d1 is 3 then maxslot = 2*nd1 + 1–2*tx = 6+1–2*tx.

Add Code 1114 to *ADDView.h*
Code 1114 Add prototypes and variables by hand to *ADDView.h*

```
void seed();                //nlp all public
long RandRange(long min, long max);
void Numbers(int nd1, int nd2);

long m_lmx1, m_lmx2; // 10^nd1, 10^nd2
long m_ln1, m_ln2;   // N1, N2
long m_lresult;      // long m_lresult,m_lanswer;

int m_nmaxslot;      // int m_npos,m_nslot,m_nmaxslot;
```

Add Code 1115 by hand to *ADDView.cpp*
Code 1115 Define and Include

```
#include <cmath>
#define RANGE(i, mn, mx) (i>=mn) && (i<mx) ? 0:1
```

Add Code 1116 to support functions in *ADDView.cpp*
Code 1116 Rand Range

```
long CADDView::RandRange(long min, long max)
{
    long int r;
    do
    {
      if (min >=10000) {r = 9 * rand();}
      else {r = rand();}
    }while (RANGE(r,min,max));
    return r;
}
```

Add Code 1117 to support functions in *ADDView.cpp*
Code 1117 Seed

```
void CADDView::seed()
{
    int utime;
    long ltime;
    ltime = time(NULL);          /* requires time.h */
    utime = (unsigned int) ltime/2;
    srand(utime);                /* requires stdlib.h */
}
```

Add Code 1118 to support functions in *ADDView.cpp*
Code 1118 Numbers

```
void CADDView::Numbers(int nd1,int nd2)
{
  m_lmx1 = (long) pow((double)10,(double)nd1);    //mx1 = 10^d1
  m_lmx2 = (long) pow((double)10,(double)nd2);    //mx2 = 10^d2

  m_ln1 = RandRange(m_lmx1/10,m_lmx1);
  m_ln2 = RandRange(m_lmx2/10,m_lmx2);
  //random selection of n1 & n2

  m_lresult = m_ln1 + m_ln2;  //will need to compare to user's answer

  int tx;    // e.g. if sum of two 3-digt numbers is xxx (tx=1) or yyyy (tx=0)
  if (m_lresult < m_lmx1) tx = 1; else tx = 0;
  m_nmaxslot = 2*nd1 + 1 – 2*tx;
}
```

11.6 How the User Solves the Problem

The user solves the problem by entering digits 0 to 9 representing sum digits and 0, 1 carry digits in defined slots (Figures 1105, 1106). The user is guided by the caret that automatically moves from slot to slot in a predefined sequence. In this way the program shows the user how to actually do the addition as defined by the *Standard Addition Algorithm with Carry* (page 106).

Figure 1105 Sum and Carry Digits

```
 0111  <--carries
 11979
+87957
------
 99936
```

Figure 1106 Slot Numbers

```
08642   < slot numbers
 40464
+59805
------
197531  < slot numbers
```

Problem display Displaying the problem requires 5 strings and a + sign (Figure 1105). The strings, actually char arrays, are for carries, number n_1, number n_2, a line under n_2, and the result (the user 's answer). A *TextOut* writes the + sign.

Add Code 1119 by hand to *ADDView.h*
Code 1119 Define and Variables

```
#define WIDTH 8       // maximum number of digits and sign allowed in a number
char m_szResult[WIDTH];
char m_szCarry[WIDTH];
char m_szLine[WIDTH];
char m_szN1[WIDTH];
char m_szN2[WIDTH];
```

Problem execution requires Screen Coordinates The user enters digits into slots marked by a program controlled caret (cursor). We need screen coordinates for the slots.

Variables *m_nxChar* and *m_nyChar* define a rectangle representing the area a digit occupies (*SelectAFont,* Code 1109 p116). The coordinates of the slot 1 rectangle (Figure 1106) are the x_0, y_0 coordinates of the first character printed on the screen by the last code line that displays the problem on the screen. *pDC -> TextOut(0,0,m_szResult)*; (Code 1121 p125)

The initial value of *m_nslot* is 1 and the initial value of *m_npos* is 0.

x coordinate The x coordinate of any column in the problem is
$$x = x0 + (m\_nd1 - m\_npos)*m\_nxChar$$

m_nd1 is the width of the number so that $x = x0 + m\_nd*m\_nxChar$ is the position of the position 0 digit. Subtract *m_npos*m_nxChar* to move the caret to the left side of the character rectangle.

y coordinate The y coordinate of the carry row in the problem is
$$y = y0 - m\_nyChar + 4*(m\_nslot\%2)*(m\_nyChar)$$

The first *m_nyChar* puts the caret at the bottom of the rectangle. In a carry slot *m_nslot%2* = 1 so that $4*(m\_nslot\%2)*(m\_nyChar)$ moves the caret into the current carry slot.

Add Code 1120 to *OnDraw* before // display etc in *ADDView.cpp*
Code 1120 Move to the current slot .See Code 1121

```
    int m_npos,m_nslot, m_nd1, m_nd2;  // add to ADDView.h
// number into current slot
    if(m_nslot<=m_nmaxslot)
    {
      pDC -> MoveTo(x0+(m_nd1 - m_npos)*m_nxChar,
          y0-m_nyChar+(m_nslot%2)*4*m_nyChar);
      pDC->SetTextAlign(TA_UPDATECP | TA_RIGHT);
      pDC->TextOut(0,0,m_nChar);

      m_ptCaretPos = pDC -> GetCurrentPosition();
      m_ptCaretPos.y += m_nyChar;
      SetCaretPos(m_ptCaretPos);
    }
```

Relation of m_npos to m_nslot

m_nslot	1	2	3	4	5	6	7
m_nslot%2	1	0	1	0	1	0	1
m_nslot− (m_nslot%2)	0	2	2	4	4	6	6
m_npos	0	1	1	2	2	3	3

Therefore m_npos = ½ [m_nslot − (m_nslot%2)]
m_nslot − (m_nslot%2)
Maximum number of slots (carry + result) The number of slots to be filled (*m_nmaxslot*) equals the number of sum digits *m_nd1* plus the number of carry digits *m_nd1* − 1, and *m_nmaxslot* = 2 *m_nd1* − 1

11.7 The Problem is Displayed on the Screen

Add Code 1121 to *OnDraw* after *CreateSolidCaret* in *ADDView.cpp*.

Code 1121 A2 code

```
    if (m_nStart==1)  // display the problem    A2
{
  SelectAFont(PROBF,pDC);
  CreateSolidCaret(m_nxChar,max(2,::GetSystemMetrics(SM_CYBORDER)));

  if (m_lresult>9)
  {
      pDC->TextOut(x0+(m_nd1+1)*m_nxChar,y0-m_nyChar,"<--carries");

      pDC->MoveTo(x0+(m_nd1 − 1)*m_nxChar,y0-m_nyChar);
      pDC->SetTextAlign(TA_UPDATECP | TA_RIGHT);
      pDC->TextOut(0,0,m_szCarry);
  }

  pDC->MoveTo(x0+(m_nd1)*m_nxChar,y0);
  pDC->SetTextAlign(TA_UPDATECP | TA_RIGHT);
  pDC->TextOut(0,0,m_szN1);

  pDC->MoveTo(x0+(m_nd1)*m_nxChar,y0+m_nyChar);
  pDC->SetTextAlign(TA_UPDATECP | TA_RIGHT);
  pDC->TextOut(0,0,m_szN2);

  pDC->MoveTo(x0-m_nxChar,y0+m_nyChar);
  pDC->SetTextAlign(TA_UPDATECP);
  pDC->TextOut(0,0,"+");

  pDC->MoveTo(x0-m_nxChar,y0+2*m_nyChar);
  pDC->SetTextAlign(TA_UPDATECP);
  pDC->TextOut(0,0,m_szLine);

  pDC->MoveTo(x0+(m_nd1)*m_nxChar,y0+3*m_nyChar);
  pDC->SetTextAlign(TA_UPDATECP | TA_RIGHT);
  pDC->TextOut(0,0,m_szResult);
```

11.8 What-to-do-next Message Handlers

After a user completes a problem message boxes appear that offer the user choices equivalent to these.

"Your answer is correct - Do you want to do a new problem?"

"Your answer is not correct - Do you want to try it again, or do you want to do a new problem?" "Do you want to quit. If no, then you can start over."

Every key press generates a *WM_CHAR* message that calls the *OnChar* function, which invokes a switch function. Key press responses are implemented by switch function cases.

Code 1122 Add variables by hand to *ADDView.h*

```
int m_ntemp;
int  m_nmsg;
int  m_nNew, m_nRepeat, m_nNewDigits, m_nQuit;
long m_lanswer;
```

Delete the code in switch(m_ni) in *OnDraw ADDView.cpp*. Then add 1123
case 1:   // select correct/not correct   break;
case 2:   // select do a new problem if not correct?   break;
case 3:   // change number of digits or quit   break;

Add Code 1123 by hand to switch(m_ni) in *OnDraw* in *ADDView.cpp*
Code 1123 Switch

```
switch(m_ni)      //process message box responses      A2 Continued
{
case 1:
  // correct/not correct
  if (m_lanswer == m_lresult)
  {
      m_nmsg=AfxMessageBox("Correct! DO A NEW PROBLEM?",MB_YESNO,0);

      switch (m_nmsg)
      {
        case IDYES:
          SendMessage(WM_CHAR,'y',0);
          SendMessage(WM_CHAR,VK_RETURN,0);
        break;
        case IDNO:
          SendMessage(WM_CHAR,'n',0);
          SendMessage(WM_CHAR,VK_RETURN,0);
        break;
      }
  }
}
```

```
        else
        {
            m_nmsg=AfxMessageBox("Not correct. TRY IT AGAIN?",MB_YESNO,0);
            switch (m_nmsg)
            {
              case IDYES:
                SendMessage(WM_CHAR,'y',0);
                SendMessage(WM_CHAR,VK_RETURN,0);
              break;

              case IDNO:
                SendMessage(WM_CHAR,'n',0);
                SendMessage(WM_CHAR,VK_RETURN,0);
              break;
            }
        }
        break;

    case 2:
        //do a new problem if not correct?
        m_nmsg=AfxMessageBox("DO A NEW PROBLEM?",MB_YESNO,0);
        switch (m_nmsg)
        {
            case IDYES:
              SendMessage(WM_CHAR,'y',0);
              SendMessage(WM_CHAR,VK_RETURN,0);
            break;
            case IDNO:
              SendMessage(WM_CHAR,'n',0);
              SendMessage(WM_CHAR,VK_RETURN,0);
            break;
        }
        break;
    case 3:
        //Change number of digits or quit
        m_nmsg=AfxMessageBox("QUIT? (on No you start over)",MB_YESNO,0);
        switch (m_nmsg)
        {
            case IDYES:
              SendMessage(WM_CHAR,'y',0);
              SendMessage(WM_CHAR,VK_RETURN,0);
            break;
            case IDNO:
              SendMessage(WM_CHAR,'n',0);
              SendMessage(WM_CHAR,VK_RETURN,0);
            break;
        }
    } //end of m_ni switch
  } //end of m_nstart==1 if
} //end of OnDraw
```

11.9 Processing User Key Press Skeleton

Code 1124 User Setup and Do The Problem Key Presses are Processed by switch functions. Do not install this code. See Codes 1125 and 1126

```
void CAddView::OnChar(UINT nChar, UINT nRepCnt, UINT nFlags)
{
    if(m_nStart==0)   //  B1
    {
      switch(nChar)
      {
        case VK_RETURN:  //Enter key
        case VK_BACK:    //Backspace key
        case 'Y':
        case 'y':
        case 'N':
        case 'n':
        case 'Q':
        case 'q':
        case '1':
        case '2':
        case '3':
        case '4':
        case '5':
        default:         // any other key - do nothing
      } //end of switch
      Invalidate(FALSE);    // redraw the screen
    }    //end of m_nstart==0 if
    else     //start of m_nstart==1   B2
    {
      switch(nChar)
      {
        case VK_RETURN:  //Enter key 1
        case VK_BACK:    //Backspace key 0
        case 'Y':  //0
        case 'y':
        case 'N':  //0
        case 'n':
        case 'Q':
        case 'q': //quit 0
        case '1':    //0
          through
        case '9':    //0
        default:   // any other key do nothing
      } //end of switch
      Invalidate(FALSE);    // redraw the screen
    }    //end of m_nstart==1 else
}
```

11.10 Processing User Setup-the-Problem Key Presses

Every key press generates a *WM_CHAR* message that calls the *OnChar* function, which includes two *switch* functions: one for problem setup and one for doing the problem. The *cases* in the *switch* functions define active keys. (Code 1124 page 128)

The *WM_CHAR* messages created by inactive keys are discarded by the switch functions.

Key presses that set up the problem:
Keys 1 to 5 The intent is for the user to press a key in the range 1 to 5 as a response to
"Select number of digits in first number: "
"Select number of digits in second number. "

User can type over digits (1 to 5) to change entries.

Nevertheless, if the user presses any sequence of keys (except Enter) only the numbers 1 to 5 will be printed. Pressing enter moves on to the next request.

Y, y User presses the y key to move on to do the problem.

N, n User presses the n key to start over.

Backspace Before enter is pressed the user can backspace to change selected values. Backspace to back up to prior steps and make changes.

Q, q User presses q to quit the program.

Enter User presses Enter to move on to the next step.
A short beep means the key pressed is inactive.
Delete this code from *OnChar* before adding code 1125
```
  if (m_nStart==0)    //  B1
  {
  }
  else    // m_nStart==1    //  B2
  {
  }
```

Add Code 1125 by hand to *OnChar* in *ADDView.cpp*
Code 1125

```
int k;          // add to OnChar ADDView.cpp
char buf[3];
UINT ch;

if(m_nStart==0)          //     B1
  {
    switch(nChar)
    {
      case VK_RETURN:   //Enter key
        m_nDigit ++;
        m_nChar =  ' ';
        m_nCharYN = ' ';

        if (m_nNew == 1)
        {
          m_ni = 0;

          if (m_nd1 < m_nd2)
          {
            m_ntemp = m_nd1;
            m_nd1 = m_nd2;
            m_nd2 = m_ntemp;

            ch = m_nChar1;
            m_nChar1 = m_nChar2;
            m_nChar2 = ch;
          }

          seed();
          Numbers(m_nd1,m_nd2);

          for(k=0;k<WIDTH;k++) m_szN1[k]= '\0';
          _ltoa(m_ln1,m_szN1,10);

          for(k=0;k<WIDTH;k++) m_szN2[k]= '\0';
          _ltoa(m_ln2,m_szN2,10);

          for(k=0;k<WIDTH;k++) m_szResult[k]= '\0';
          for(k=0;k<m_nd1;k++) m_szResult[k]= ' ';

          for(k=0;k<WIDTH;k++) m_szCarry[k]= '\0';
          for(k=0;k<m_nd1;k++) m_szCarry[k]= ' ';

          for(k=0;k<WIDTH;k++) m_szLine[k]= '\0';
          for(k=0;k<m_nd1+1;k++) m_szLine[k]= '-';

          m_nStart = 1;
          m_nslot = 1;
```

```
      m_npos = 0;
    }
    m_nNew = 0;

    if (m_nRepeat == 1)
    {
      m_nDigit = 1;
      m_nChar1 = ' ';
      m_nChar2 = ' ';
    }
    m_nRepeat = 0;

    if (m_nDigit > 3)
    {
      m_nDigit = 1;
    }

    break;

case VK_BACK:      //Backspace key  0
    if (m_nDigit>1)
    {
      m_nDigit--;
      m_nChar =  ' ';
      m_nCharYN = ' ';
      m_nNew = 0;
    }
    else
    {
      MessageBeep((WORD) − 1);
    }
    break;

case 'Y':   //0
case 'y':
    if (m_nDigit<3) MessageBeep((WORD) − 1);

    if (m_nDigit>=3)
    {
      m_nCharYN = nChar;
      m_nNew = 1;
      m_nRepeat = 0;
    }
    break;
```

```
      case 'N':  //0
      case 'n':
        if (m_nDigit<3) MessageBeep((WORD) − 1);

        if (m_nDigit>=3)
        {
          m_nCharYN = nChar;
          m_nRepeat = 1;  //start problem setup over
          m_nNew = 0;
        }
        break;

      case 'Q':
      case 'q': //quit 0
        exit(0);
        break;

      case '1':   //0
      case '2':   //0
      case '3':   //0
      case '4':   //0
      case '5':   //0
        if (m_nDigit==1)
        {
          m_nChar1 = nChar;
          buf[0] = (char) nChar;
          m_nd1 = atoi(buf);
        }

        if (m_nDigit==2)
        {
          m_nChar2 = nChar;
          buf[0] = (char) nChar;
          m_nd2 = atoi(buf);
        }
        break;

      default: //0  any other char do nothing
      MessageBeep((WORD) − 1);

  } //end of switch

  Invalidate(FALSE);   // redraw the screen

} //end of m_nstart==0 if
```

11.11 Processing User Do-the-Problem Key Presses

Every key press generates a *WM_CHAR* message that calls the *OnChar* function, which includes two *switch* functions: one for problem setup and one for doing the problem. The *cases* in the *switch* functions define active keys.

The *WM_CHAR* messages created by inactive keys are discarded by the switch functions.

Key presses setting up the problem:
Keys 0 to 9 The intent is for the user to press a key in the range 0 to 9 as a sum digit in a slot or 0 to 1 as a carry digit in a slot.

User can type over digits (0 to 9) to change entries.

User does not have to enter the carries. Press Enter to skip over.

Nevertheless, if the user presses any sequence of keys (except Enter) only the numbers 0 to 9 will be printed. Pressing enter moves on to the next slot.

Y, y User presses the y key to respond to the message.

N, n User presses the n key to respond to the message.

Q, q User presses q to quit the program.

Backspace Before enter is pressed the user can backspace to change sum digit or carry digit values. Backspace to back up to prior steps and make changes.

Enter User presses Enter to move on to the next step.

A short beep means the key you pressed is inactive.

Add Code 1126 by hand to *OnChar* in *ADDView.cpp*
Code 1126

```
else //start of m_nstart==1      //  B2
  {
    switch(nChar)
    {
      case VK_RETURN:   //Enter key 1
        // go to next slot
        m_nslot++;
        m_npos = (m_nslot − (m_nslot%2))/2;
        m_nChar = ' ';

        // is problem done?
        if ((m_ni==0) && (m_nslot==m_nmaxslot+1))
        {
          m_ni=1; //problem done
          m_lanswer = atol(m_szResult);
        }

        // new problem with same number of digits
        if (m_nNew == 1)
        {
          Numbers(m_nd1,m_nd2);

          for(k=0;k<WIDTH;k++) m_szN1[k]= '\0';
          _ltoa(m_ln1,m_szN1,10);

          for(k=0;k<WIDTH;k++) m_szN2[k]= '\0';
          _ltoa(m_ln2,m_szN2,10);
        }
        m_nNew = 0;

        // repeat current problem
        if (m_nRepeat == 1)
        {
          m_ni=0;
          m_nslot = 1;
          m_npos = 0;

          for(k=0;k<WIDTH;k++) m_szResult[k]= '\0';
          for(k=0;k<m_nd1;k++) m_szResult[k]= ' ';

          for(k=0;k<WIDTH;k++) m_szCarry[k]= '\0';
          for(k=0;k<m_nd1;k++) m_szCarry[k]= ' ';
        }
        m_nRepeat = 0;
```

```
  // new problem with new numbers of digits
  if (m_nNewDigits==1)
  {
    m_nStart = 0;
    m_nDigit = 1;
    m_nslot = 1;
    m_npos = 0;
  }
  m_nNewDigits = 0;

  if (m_nQuit==1)
  {
    exit(0);
  }

  break;

case VK_BACK:    //Backspace key  1
  if ((m_ni==0) && (m_nslot>1))
  {
    m_nslot--;
    m_npos = (m_nslot − (m_nslot%2))/2;
    m_nChar = ' ';
  }
  else
  {
    MessageBeep((WORD) − 1);
  }
  break;

case 'Y':
case 'y': //  1
  if (m_ni==0) MessageBeep((WORD) − 1);

  switch(m_ni)
  {
  case 1:
    //not correct, try again
    if (m_lanswer != m_lresult)
    {
      m_nRepeat = 1;
    }

    //correct, do new problem
    if (m_lanswer == m_lresult)
    {
      m_nNew = 1;
      m_nRepeat = 1;
    }
    break;
```

```
    case 2:
      //not correct, do new problem
      if (m_lanswer!=m_lresult)
      {
        m_nNew = 1;
        m_nRepeat = 1;
      }
      break;

    case 3:
      // quit
      m_nQuit = 1;
      break;
    }
    break;

case 'N':
case 'n':    // 1
    //do nothing
    if (m_ni==0) MessageBeep((WORD) - 1);

    switch(m_ni)
    {
    case 1:
      //not correct,do not try again
      if (m_lanswer != m_lresult)
      {
        m_ni = 2;
        m_nNew = 0;
        m_nRepeat = 0;
        m_nNewDigits = 0;
      }

      //correct, do not do new problem
      if (m_lanswer == m_lresult)
      {
        m_ni = 3;
        m_nNew = 0;
        m_nRepeat = 0;
        m_nNewDigits = 0;
      }
      break;

    case 2:
      //not correct, do not do new problem
      if (m_lanswer!=m_lresult)
      {
        m_ni = 3;
        m_nNew = 0;
        m_nRepeat = 0;
        m_nNewDigits = 0;
      }
```

```
          break;

      case 3:

          // do new problem with new numbers of digits
          m_nNewDigits = 1;
          m_nQuit = 0;
          break;

      } //end of switch m_ni
      break;

    case 'Q':
    case 'q': //quit 1
      exit(0);
      break;

    case '0':    //1
    case '1':    //1
    case '2':    //1
    case '3':    //1
    case '4':    //1
    case '5':    //1
    case '6':    //1
    case '7':    //1
    case '8':    //1
    case '9':    //1
      if(m_ni==0)
      {
        m_nChar = nChar;
        if (m_nslot%2)
        {
          m_szResult[m_nd1 - m_npos] = (char) nChar;
        }
        else
        {
          m_szCarry[m_nd1 - m_npos] = (char) nChar;
        }
      }
      break;

    default:
      MessageBeep((WORD) - 1);
    } //end of switch else
    Invalidate();   // redraw the problem only

  } //end of m_nstart==1 else

  CView::OnChar(nChar, nRepCnt, nFlags);
} // end of OnChar
```

11.12 A Simple Help Function

This is the simple help system. A right mouse click accesses it (JP102).

This is for a mouse action
Click on *View*, click on *Class Wizard*, click on *Message Maps*.
Verify Project is *ADD*, Class name is *CADDView*.
In the *Object Ids* box click on *ADDView*
In the *Messages* box click on   *WM_RButtonDown*.
Click on *Add Function* to add *OnRButtonDown*
Click on *Edit Code* to see function added as a skeleton message handler.
Add following code to the message handler.

Add Code 1127 to support functions in *ADDView.cpp*.
Code 1127 OnRButtonDown

```
void CAddView::OnRButtonDown(UINT nFlags, CPoint point)
{
  // TODO: Add your message handler code here and/or call default

  CString strRightClick ;

  strRightClick = (CString)
      "Use keyboard to enter numbers; press Enter to continue."
    + "\n\n"
    + "The maximum number of digits is 5"
    + "\n"
    + "Can quit anytime (use keys: q,Q)"
    + "\n"
    + "Can type over numbers (0 to 9) to change your entries."
    + "\n"
    + "You do not have to enter the carries. Press Enter to skip over."
    + "\n"
    + "Press Enter to proceed to the next step."
    + "\n"
    + "Press Backspace to back up to prior step and make changes."
    + "\n"
    + "Respond to requests with yes or no (use keys: y,Y,n,N)"
    + "\n"
    + "A short beep means the key you pressed is inactive";

  MessageBox(strRightClick,
        "Active Keys: Enter, Backspace, q, Q, y, Y, n, N, 0 to 9",
        MB_OK);
  CView::OnRButtonDown(nFlags, point);
}
```

11.13 Variable Definitions and Initial Values

Here are all of the variables and prototypes used in the *ADD* program.
DO NOT add to *ADDView.h.* **This is a recap, however see Code 1130.**

Code 1128 Variable and Prototype Definitions added to *ADDView.h*

```
#define WIDTH 8
// Overrides  (added in Section 11.1)
public:
virtual void OnDraw(CDC* pDC);  // overridden to draw this view   //nlp
virtual void OnInitialUpdate();

// Generated message map functions
protected:
  //{{AFX_MSG(CAddView)  //nlp
  afx_msg void OnChar(UINT nChar, UINT nRepCnt, UINT nFlags);
  afx_msg void OnKillFocus(CWnd* pNewWnd);
  afx_msg void OnRButtonDown(UINT nFlags, CPoint point);
  afx_msg void OnSetFocus(CWnd* pOldWnd);
  //}}AFX_MSG

private:
  UINTm_nChar1, m_nChar2, m_nChar, m_nCharYN;
  CPoint  m_ptCaretPos;
  int  m_nxChar, m_nyChar;

public:
  void seed();
  void SelectAFont(int n,CDC* pDC);
  long RandRange(long min, long max);
  void Numbers(int nd1, int nd2);

  long m_lmx1, m_lmx2;   //10^nd1, 10^nd2
  long m_ln1, m_ln2;   // N1, N2
  long m_lresult,m_lanswer;

  int m_nd1,m_nd2;     // number of digits in N1,N2
  int m_nStart,m_nDigit,m_ntemp;
  int m_npos,m_nslot,m_nmaxslot;
  int m_nmsg, m_ni;
  int m_nNew, m_nRepeat, m_nNewDigits, m_nQuit;
  char m_szResult[WIDTH];
  char m_szCarry[WIDTH];
  char m_szLine[WIDTH];
  char m_szN1[WIDTH];
  char m_szN2[WIDTH];
  CFont* m_pOldFont;
```

OnInitialUpdate() initializes all variables.

Code 1129 Variable Initial Values added to *ADDView.cpp*

```
// TO BE ADDED AS CODE IS ENTERED IN THE FOLLOWING PAGES

void CAddView::OnInitialUpdate()
{
  CView::OnInitialUpdate();

  // TODO: Add your specialized code here and/or call the base class
  m_nNew = 0;
  m_nRepeat = 0;
  m_nNewDigits= 0;
  m_nQuit = 0;
  m_nStart = 0;
  m_nDigit = 1;
  m_nslot = 1;
  m_npos = 0;
  m_ni = 0;
  m_nmsg = 0;
  m_nd1 = 1;
  m_nd2 = 1;
  m_nChar1 = ' ';
  m_nChar2 = ' ';
  m_nChar = ' ';
  m_nCharYN = ' ';
}
```

Add Code 1130 to *OnInitialUpdate in ADDview.cpp*.
Code 1130 Initialized variables

```
m_nNew = 0;
m_nRepeat = 0;
m_nNewDigits= 0;
m_nQuit = 0;
m_nslot = 1;
m_npos = 0;
m_ni = 0;
m_nmsg = 0;
m_nd1 = 1;
m_nd2 = 1;
```

Index